"*You kn*

*know much,*

Susan quipped. "I mean that if you want to catch Kyle, you're going to have to play hard to get. Stop sitting near him and talking to him. Let him come to you."

"What if he doesn't?" Rachel's voice betrayed her uncertainty.

"Then you move on." Susan put an arm around her shoulders. "You can't go on waiting for something that may never happen. Give him lots of space and widen your horizons. Go out with Jason."

Rachel groaned. "Not Jason again. He is so totally not my type."

"Well then, somebody. Anybody," Susan said, throwing her hands up in the air. "You never know. It might wake Kyle up to what he's missing."

Rachel thought it over—it might just do that. But she hated the thought of using someone else to get Kyle to notice her. She would just play hard to get. If someone else asked her out. . .well, there was no reason she couldn't say yes. After all, she wasn't exactly committed to Kyle. She thought it over. Who would she go out with? Her acquaintances were pretty limited. She spent most of her time either at the community center or at the university. Just then Dr. Harris's face flashed across her mind, but was quickly extinguished. Like he would ever ask her out.

**LINDA LYLE** hails from Alabama. She is an avid reader who became interested in writing in the eighth grade and keeps an extensive journal of ideas. Linda is very happy to be able to write wholesome, entertaining fiction that portrays her Christian values.

**Books by Linda Lyle**

HEARTSONG PRESENTS
HP278—Elizabeth's Choice

Don't miss out on any of our super romances. Write to us at the following address for information on our newest releases and club information.

Heartsong Presents Readers' Service
PO Box 719
Uhrichsville, OH 44683

# The Plan

*Linda Lyle*

Heartsong Presents

To Jeanette and Jackie Johnson,
who taught me to look for God's plan in my life.

**A note from the author:**
*I love to hear from my readers! You may correspond with me by writing:*
**Linda Lyle**
**Author Relations**
**PO Box 719**
**Uhrichsville, OH 44683**

**ISBN 1-57748-630-7**

**THE PLAN**



Scripture quotations marked KJV are taken from the King James Version of the Bible.

All of the characters and events in this book are fictitious. Any resemblance to actual persons, living or dead, or to actual events is purely coincidental.

*Cover illustration by Victoria Lisi and Julius.*

PRINTED IN THE U.S.A.

# one

The snow fell in soft clusters onto the already saturated ground, but clumps of brown grass stuck out in odd intervals. Rachel used these like stepping stones, stretching from one clump of brown to another in a vain attempt to keep her new shoes clean. Despite of the mud, she hummed a little tune. There was nothing like snow to make even the worst day seem special.

She left the mud and snow behind as she climbed the crumbling stairs. The sign proclaiming "Myerstown Community Center" hung lopsided and creaked in the wind. Rachel gave one last shiver as another blast bit through her wool coat. She had made a dash for the door that clanged shut behind her, the echo following her down the hall. She hurried as fast as she could with her heavy bag to Room 102, and as she feared, her students were already assembled.

"Good morning. Sorry I'm late," Rachel said between breaths.

"Good morning," said Mrs. Lee. "Why are you breathing so hard?"

"I had to walk from the bus station."

"Why were you riding the bus? Where's your car?" asked Mrs. Martinez.

"It's in the shop."

"In the shop," Mrs. Sato said, forming the words carefully. "What does that mean?"

"I'm sorry. I'm talking in slang again. That means my car isn't working and I took it to a mechanic to be repaired."

Mrs. Sato's eyes lit in understanding and a wave of "ahs" passed through the room. "So a shop is a place for repairing things, yes?"

"That's right," Rachel said as she pulled book after book from her bag. It was like Mary Poppins's magic carpetbag—there never seemed to be a bottom. "Let's work on chapter three. We will begin with vocabulary pronunciation. Repeat after me. Valuable." There was a general murmur of incoherent sounds. "One more time. Val-u-a-ble." Rachel continued down the list, stopping and repeating when they struggled.

They spent the next half hour doing substitution drills and sentence drills, using the new vocabulary. At the break, Rachel left them to their coffee and snacks and went down the hall to the office. Susan was not at her desk, so Rachel wound her way to the supply room at the back.

"Susan. . . ." A squeal stopped her in midsentence.

"You scared me half to death! Don't sneak up on me like that!"

"I'm sorry I scared you, but I wasn't sneaking. I walked across the room like any normal person."

"I'm going to put a bell around your neck, so I'll know

you're coming." Susan walked backed to her desk, one hand still over her heart. She sat down at her desk, took a deep breath, and then turned back. "Now. What did you want?"

"I need some help. I've gotten a request to start a citizenship class, as well as another conversational English class."

"I know. I know. I've been beating the bushes for more teachers, but all I got was splinters. Everybody is busy, or doesn't think they are qualified, or they just don't care."

"Well, I'm busy and I teach and the only qualification is that I speak good English and care about people. As far as the last part, I can't help you with that." Rachel shrugged and sank into the chair across from Susan. "What are we going to do?"

"The only option left is to pray," Susan said.

"That should have been our first priority."

"I know, but where are we going to find more teachers? Besides that, the stairs are crumbling, the leak is roofing. . ."

"Wait a minute," Rachel interrupted, "you mean the roof is leaking."

"No. There is definitely more leak than roof at this point." They both laughed, but quickly sobered when they realized the truth in the statement. "We need a miracle."

"Well, I guess we'll just have to pray for one," Rachel said resolutely.

"How can you be so sure?"

"I know God can do all things. You just have to have faith."

"Easier said than done," Susan replied. "Speaking of faith, how's your man?"

"He's not 'my man' and he's as annoying as usual." Rachel plucked imaginary fuzz off her skirt. She could feel the blood rushing to her face at just the mention of Kyle.

"Likely story." Susan smiled.

Rachel knew that she couldn't hide it from Susan, but she wasn't going to admit it either. She felt like a fool as it was. She didn't need any extra help from Susan. As soon as she felt recovered, she looked up at her friend, head cocked. "I don't want to talk about him."

"Fine, fine, but let's talk about somebody. You need to get out more. You're not getting any younger."

"Here we go again. I'm not that old, and I don't appreciate your acting like I am. Twenty-nine is not that old."

"I know, but at the rate you're going you'll never get married. You've got to quit waiting around for Kyle. You know he's not interested. He's made it clear in a hundred ways. Let me set you up with Jason. He's a great guy."

"No thank you. I don't need your help to get a date. Besides, I've seen what you drag up."

"That's not fair. Tommy was a nice guy. You didn't give him a chance."

"Sure, he's a nice guy, but he's not interested in church or anything that has to do with it. What would I do with a guy like that?" Rachel asked.

"Go out and have a good time, instead of sitting at home alone every weekend."

"I happen to like a little quiet time. There's nothing wrong with staying home on Friday or Saturday night. You've been watching too much TV."

"Come on, Rachel. Let me set you up with Jason. Give him a chance. You never know what might happen."

"I know. That's what I'm afraid of." Susan made a face and threw a paper wad across the desk. Rachel caught it and threw it right back. "I'll let God do the picking. I trust His judgment."

"Thanks for your support," Susan said, rolling her eyes. "I'll remember that the next time you come crying to me for advice."

"Yeah, yeah. I'm so worried." Rachel got up and moved toward the door.

"Well, you don't have to leave. I was only joking."

"I know, but break time is over. Back to the trenches."

By the time class was finished, Rachel felt like an almost empty coffeepot, drained and cloudy. She gathered up her papers, stuck them in the already overflowing bag, and heaved it onto her thin shoulder. Just as she swung it into place, a lock of her hair fell underneath the strap, giving her hair a good yank. She muttered as she struggled to free her hair from the weight, but she finally had to yank it loose. Dark strands of hair fell and attached themselves to her white sweater. As she plucked the hairs from her sweater, she noticed something shining in the light. She held it to the light, thinking it was a fiber from her sweater.

"Oh, no! It can't be!" she moaned. She ran to the mirror and looked again. Sure enough, she was holding her first gray hair in her hand. Not just gray. It was silver and shiny. Her face fell as Susan's words rang in her ears.

*You're not getting any younger. You're not getting any younger. You're not getting any younger. . .*

"Stop it," Rachel squealed, stomping her feet.

"What?" Susan called from the hall.

"Nothing. I was talking to myself."

"Great. The first thing to go is the mind. I was right. You're well on your way over that hill." Susan smiled as she said it, but the words stung.

"Gee, thanks. With a friend like you who needs enemies?" The words came out a little sharper than she intended, so Rachel smiled to soften the blow. Susan only made a silly face and stuck out her tongue before continuing down the hall.

Rachel grabbed her bag and strode out into the crisp air, but the snow didn't lift her spirits this time. That silver hair had made more of an impact than she was willing to face right then. She tried to put it out of her mind as she headed toward the university. The bus ride was crowded and stifling. By the time she got off in front of Bowden Hall, she was ready for the stiff breeze. Each time she climbed the steps, she was struck by the inequality of it all. Here was this architectural masterpiece with its spacious halls and polished wood floors while across town the community center was quickly falling into decay. Both buildings were built before the turn of the century. Why was this one chosen to flourish and the other to crumble slowly into pieces? She shook her head at the injustice. Entering the building, she made her way to the third floor. It seemed she was destined to work on the third floor of buildings with no elevators. This one did have an elevator, but it was so small that she got claustrophobic every time she went near it. She would rather climb the three flights and be free to move, than ride in that deathtrap. She topped the last stair, gasping for breath, right outside Dr. Harris's office. He stuck his head out, a dark wave of hair falling across his forehead.

"Are you all right?" he asked. She held up her hands as she caught her breath. He smoothed the lock back into place with slender fingers. Watching his hands, Rachel was surprised that there was no ring. He seemed like the type to settle down. Someone so handsome and intelligent should have his pick of women. The touch of gray at his temples only added to his charm. She shook off the thought. It was really none of her business anyway. She took a deep breath before she answered him.

"I'm fine, Dr. Harris. I'm just out of shape. These stairs will kill you," she said with a half laugh, half gasp.

"Why don't you take the elevator?"

"I like breathing."

"Obviously." They both laughed. "Where are you off to today?"

"English 101, otherwise known as Freshman Torture."

He chuckled. "I never heard it put exactly that way, but that's pretty good."

"I guess I'd better move along while I'm still able. I'll see you around, Dr. Harris."

"By the way, you don't have to call me Dr. Harris anymore. You're an instructor, too, now. Why don't you call me Randy?"

"It's a hard habit to break." It was true. There was probably only a few years difference in their ages, but it was hard to imagine calling him by his first name. She moved thc bag onto her hip. "I'd better get going or I'll be late." She waved and walked on down the hall. Ten minutes later she was deep into her review of basic grammar and Dr. Harris was not even a memory.

# two

Randall Harris watched until Rachel turned the corner. With a sigh he turned back to the papers he was grading, but he couldn't concentrate. He was beginning to wonder if he was losing it. Spending his days daydreaming about her could get him into trouble. It was a bit of a quandary. Here he was a nice, single professor surrounded by nice, single young women. The only problem was they were all his students. He was only five years older than some of his students, yet it was career suicide to date any one of them. Rachel, on the other hand, was not a student anymore, but they were still separated by that teacher/student relationship, a self-imposed distance. In trying to protect himself, he had separated himself from the one woman who really interested him.

When he went home that night, she followed him home in his thoughts. He put his hand on his head and rested his elbows on his desk. Looking around his cluttered living room, he felt the emptiness. In the midst of all the junk he had accumulated in the last ten years, he felt as if the room were bare. "God, I don't know what to do," he whispered. "I'm so lonely right now." He had made a habit of taking his troubles to the Lord years ago, but tonight it seemed his prayer was hitting the ceiling and bouncing back like an echo. "I know You said that You are all we need, but You also saw Adam's need for a mate. That's why You sent Eve. Why should I be any different?" He raked his hands through his hair and rested his head on the desk. Tears burned his eyes, but refused to be shed. He was a grown man, and men didn't cry.

*"Jesus cried."*

*What?*

*"Jesus cried."*

The tears came then, a release of the emotions pent up inside. The tears opened the barriers and allowed God's calming presence to wrap him in a cloak of love. He dried his eyes and bowed his head once more.

"Now what, Lord?"

*"Wait on me. Hear my Word."*

He picked up his Bible and it fell open to Proverbs 19:21. "There are many devices in a man's heart; nevertheless the counsel of the Lord, that shall stand." He looked down at the footnote, which read, "Devices means plans."

"Lord, I know you have a plan for my life. Is Rachel a part of that plan? Or is that just wishful thinking?"

There was no answer, only a hush. He waited a few more moments, but sensed that the Spirit had finished speaking for now. He went to bed only to toss and turn, finally drifting off to a vision of Rachel holding a baby that looked curiously like him.

❧

Rachel spent the evening staring at the back of Kyle's head. She tried to memorize every line and feature. From his sandy brown hair and green eyes to his crooked smile, he was perfect. It took everything she had not to sigh out loud. He kept his back turned to her during the whole service and muttered a good-bye as he headed for the opposite side of the room as fast as his long legs would carry him. She watched him until he disappeared through the side door.

"Could you be a little more obvious?"

"What? Oh, hey, Susan."

"Well it's great to see you too. How was your day? It was great. How about you?" Susan said, carrying on a conversation with herself.

"Sorry," Rachel said.

"Yeah, right," Susan said, cocking her head sideways. "I really believe it."

Rachel threw a playful punch. "If I didn't know you any better, I would think you were jealous."

"Jealous of what? A make-believe romance? Hardly."

"No need to rub it in."

"Just forget him. There are lots of great guys out there who are dying to go out with you."

"Yeah right. They're knocking down my door. That's why I haven't had a date in five years."

"Whose fault is that?" Susan asked, hands on hips.

"What do you mean?"

"What do I mean? I mean that no guy is going to ask

you out while you're following Kyle around like a puppy dog, especially not Kyle."

"What do you mean?"

"You know for such a smart girl, you sure don't know much," Susan quipped. "I mean that if you want to catch Kyle, you're going to have to play hard to get. Stop sitting near him and talking to him. Let him come to you."

"What if he doesn't?" Rachel's voice betrayed her uncertainty.

"Then you move on." Susan put an arm around her shoulders. "You can't go on waiting for something that may never happen. Give him lots of space and widen your horizons. Go out with Jason."

Rachel groaned. "Not Jason again. He is so totally not my type."

"Well then, somebody. Anybody," Susan said, throwing her hands up in the air. "You never know. It might wake Kyle up to what he's missing."

Rachel thought it over—it might just do that. But she hated the thought of using someone else to get Kyle to notice her. She would just play hard to get. If someone else asked her out. . .well, there was no reason she couldn't say yes. After all, she wasn't exactly committed to Kyle. She thought it over. Who would she go out with? Her acquaintances were pretty limited. She spent most of her time either at the community center or at the university. Just then Dr. Harris's face flashed across her mind, but was quickly extinguished. Like he would ever ask her out.

"Are you sleepwalking? I asked if you were ready to go," Susan called.

"I'm coming."

Rachel thought all night and most of the rest of the week about what Susan had said. It made sense. Men liked what they couldn't have. She made a decision that night to put a plan into action. Sunday she would sit across the church from Kyle, and she wouldn't talk to him. She would pretend she couldn't see him at all. It was going to take all the self-control she possessed and more. This was going to take more than she had. But she was determined. The decision made, she rolled over and tried to get to sleep. Pushing images of Kyle out of her mind, she drifted off to sleep, but just before dawn Randall Harris crept into her dreams and then vanished with the sunrise.

# three

The next morning dawned bright and blue without a trace of snow. Alabama weather could really throw a person. A couple of days ago she was trudging through the snow and today she was tempted to wear a T-shirt and shorts. It was definitely spring. Rachel skipped across the quad in high spirits. Susan's suggestion had given her a spark of hope—something she hadn't had in a long time. She still wasn't sure how to pull it off, but she was working on it. She just had to keep her eyes open for any opportunity to put the plan into action. With a smile and a whistle she bounded up the stairs to her classroom.

❧

Randy watched her pass. Her smile literally took his breath away. It took several seconds to slow down the thumping of his heart. Many times when she had been in his class he had found it hard to concentrate on the lecture when she smiled that smile. He opened and closed his pen ten times and then began to beat a rhythm on his desk. His roaming eyes fell on a flyer that had been buried under a pile of papers. Pulling it from the stack, he ignored the avalanche that slid onto the floor. Here was the answer to his dilemma. All he had to do was catch her on her way out of class. This would be the place to start.

Randy positioned his chair so he could watch for Rachel, holding a copy of *The Canterbury Tales* as if deep in the story—though any passerby wouldn't have been fooled because he was holding the book upside-down. Fortunately he put it aside before Rachel had a clear view.

"Rachel, I'm so glad you came by today."

"I always come by on Monday afternoon. I have a class. Remember?" Rachel's smile widened, and her eyes twinkled.

"Of course. Of course. I had forgotten." That was a lie. He had looked her schedule up on the computer and had committed it to memory. When he paused, Rachel gently nudged him.

"What did you want?"

"Oh, yes. I–I wanted to ask. . .or actually tell you about this." He pulled the flyer off his desk, sending his pen and a bottle of Coke rolling to the floor. Luckily the cap was still on the bottle. He rushed to pick them up and threw them onto the chair. Rachel looked as if she were suppressing a laugh. He handed her the flyer announcing that a local historian would be speaking this evening on the history of some local buildings. "I know you have an interest in history and architecture from the presentation on the Victorian era that you did in class. I thought we might walk over together."

Randy knew that Rachel loved learning about history,

especially architecture—he could see it in the way her eyes sparkled whenever the topic came up. "That would be great. When did you want to go? This says the presentation doesn't start for another hour."

"I was just about to go to The Magnolia for some coffee. Would you care to join me?" He tried to sound casual, but his erratic heartbeat was making it hard to breathe.

"Sure, that would be great. That way I won't have to lug this bag around all over the place." Rachel smiled, patting the bag like a puppy.

"Well, just let me lock up and we'll be on our way." He picked up his briefcase and jacket and searched for his keys. Rachel tapped him on the shoulder and moved past him.

"They're right here, professor." Thankfully, she kept her smile from breaking out in laughter, causing small dimples in her cheeks to appear.

"Oh, yes. Right where I left them. Thank you." The keys jingled as he tried to find the right key on the ring and then locked the door. "Okay. Let's go."

They walked across the quad in companionable silence, taking in the budding trees and blooming flowerbeds. He held the door open for her when they reached The Magnolia. He picked out a table in the corner which overlooked the quad. When the waitress came, Rachel ordered an amaretto cappuccino.

"You like cappuccino?" At her nod, Randy continued, "So do I, but I prefer French vanilla." The waitress wrote down his order and disappeared behind the counter. The cafe was fairly busy for this time of day with people scattered throughout the room. Randy was looking around, trying to think of something to say when her bag caught his eye.

"What do you keep in that thing anyway?"

"This is what I call my portable office." She pulled a chair out and heaved the bag into the seat. Opening the front flap revealed a series of little compartments. "Here you have your red pen, blue pen, black pen and a lavender pen for those color-sensitive students. Then, you have your sticky notes, calculator, ruler, and stapler. I also have chalk, dry erase markers, and scissors. You never know what you'll need."

"Wow. A veritable stationery store." His face relaxed into a smile.

"That's not all."

"No?"

"No." She unzipped a large section and pulled back the sides so he could see. "You have your dictionary, grammar guide, thesaurus, textbooks, and various student papers."

"How much does all that weigh?" he asked, his eyes bulging in fascination.

"I don't want to know. I do know that it's giving my arms a workout." They both laughed.

Talk turned to students and grading. They swapped ideas and lesson plans. After the waitress brought their order, they discussed literature and books in general.

They had a lot in common, except he preferred modern and she Victorian. Looking down at her watch, Rachel said, "We'd better hurry or we'll be late." She swallowed the last of her coffee and closed up her bag.

"Fashionably late."

"As an English teacher you should know that there is no such thing as fashionably late. It's just plain late." He threw back his head and laughed.

"You are very good with words," he said. He could see a blush rise on her cheeks at the compliment.

"Thank you very much, kind sir," she said, giving a mock curtsy. "I had an excellent teacher." He inclined his head in gracious approval and offered his arm.

In an exaggerated Southern accent, he said, "May I escort the lady across the lawn?"

She took his arm with a solemn smile. "You most certainly may." They had gone only a few feet when they both burst out laughing.

Randy's spirits soared as he walked across the campus with Rachel on his arm. It was the first time in a long time that he had had this much fun. After the first awkward moments were over, it seemed they had been friends for ages.

During the presentation, he spent more time watching Rachel than listening to the speaker. He loved watching the sparkle and intensity in her face as she made notes on what the speaker was saying. Her love of learning was one of the things that had instantly attracted him. Tonight he realized that she was witty and funny.

Now, more than ever, he wanted to get to know her on a personal basis.

❧

Rachel listened to the speaker intently. Her ears had picked up at the mention of the community center. Dr. Miller was telling how the building had once been the town library, but it had been damaged in the Civil War. A new library had been built across town, leaving the building empty for several years. It had been used for various things over the years until it had been donated as a community center.

When the speaker moved on to talk about the post office, Rachel stole a glance at her companion. There was more to Dr. Harris than she had imagined. He had a wonderful sense of humor and a way of listening to what she said that made her feel special and interesting. No one had ever paid this much attention to what she had to say before, even when they were discussing literature. Kyle never. . .well, she wouldn't think about that now. She had vowed she would ignore him and make him see what he was missing. Other men found her intelligent. Although she suspected the professor was just being nice.

Just then their eyes met and he smiled. Her heart gave a funny flutter. It must have been the excitement of the evening. She felt the blood warm her cheeks, and she turned back to the speaker to hide her embarrassment.

Dr. Miller left the stage to applause, and everyone stood. Rachel stretched like a cat. "I can never get comfortable in these seats."

"I know what you mean." Dr. Harris pressed his hands into the small of his back with a frown. Rachel's stomach let out a growl, causing her face to glow and the professor to smile. Talking to her stomach, he said, "That's a good idea. Dinner would be just the thing."

"I'm sorry. I'm keeping you from your dinner."

"No such thing. It sounds more like I'm keeping you from yours," he said, laughing.

"Well, I didn't have much lunch because I was late getting out of my other class. One of the students needed some extra help."

"Then I guess I owe you dinner. Shall we?" He held out his arm again. "I know a quaint little Italian place within walking distance." He pointed to her bag. "We could share the load."

"There's really no need. I can just go home and grab a bite."

"Nonsense. I'd like the company."

"Well, if it's not a bother."

He picked up her bag with a mock groan and then offered her his arm. Despite his reference to sharing the load, he carried the bag all the way to the restaurant. After a delicious dinner, he insisted on walking her to her door, only relinquishing the bag once they were under the porch light.

"Thanks for dinner and for carrying my bag," she said, pulling at the strap.

"Thank you. I enjoyed it very much. Maybe we can do it again sometime."

"Maybe."

"Good night, Rachel."

"Good night, Dr. Harris."

"Do you have to call me that? My name's Randy."

"I'll try to remember, but old habits are hard to break." He smiled and waved good-bye as he turned to go. She watched him with mixed feelings. The evening had been wonderful, but what did he mean by doing this again? Was he talking about a date? A feeling of excitement welled up inside her, but she wasn't sure why. Was it the fact that her plan was starting to work without any effort on her part? Or that she really liked Dr. Harris. . . Randy?

❧

Randy whistled his way home. The smile never left his face. He had taken the first step in his plan and things were going well. The next step was to get her to stop calling him Dr. Harris. He took the stairs to his Victorian house two at a time. For once, coming home was a pleasure, not a prison sentence. He had bought this house with the hopes of filling it with a family. As a year passed, the house itself seemed to mock his loneliness. His plans for the house had ceased to thrill him, and he had left several projects undone. He was realizing just how depressed and defeated he had become. He walked through the house, seeing it with new eyes. Inspiration and energy seemed to pump through his blood. He went inside and changed clothes and then starting stripping the parlor floor with enthusiasm. It was sometime after one o'clock before he went to bed, still whistling a tune. One day he would have that family—maybe with Rachel.

# four

The air was warm and a restless wind was blowing Rachel's hair into her eyes. April in Alabama was as unpredictable as a wild animal. In spite of the muggy weather, she shook off a shiver and quickened her steps across the lawn. The Center's sign creaked in the breeze, reminding her of a ghost town in a western.

"Hey! What are you grinning at?" Susan called from the doorway.

"Nothing."

"Well that's a pretty big grin to be nothing. You're not thinking about Kyle, are you?"

"Nope," she answered honestly. "He was the furthest thing from my mind until you mentioned him."

"That's progress! Maybe there is hope for you yet."

"Maybe so. I've got a shocker for you," Rachel said with a grin. "You'll never believe it, not in a million billion years."

"Well, don't keep me in suspense," Susan said, hands on hips. "Spit it out!"

Rachel just smiled for a few minutes until Susan looked fit to explode. "I, Rachel Grant, had a. . .date." She watched as Susan's eyes popped open and her jaw dropped to the step. "Yes, you heard it right. I had a date with an eligible male last night whose first name was not Kyle."

Susan ran down the stairs squealing and shaking her until she was almost deaf. "When? Who? What?"

"Whoa, slow down. This isn't the Spanish Inquisition." Rachel chuckled. "When? Last night. Who? Dr. Harris. What? A cappuccino, a lecture, and dinner."

"I can't believe it." Susan was still squealing and several passersby stared. "Let's go inside where we're not so obvious." Susan yanked her toward the stairs.

"*We?* What do you mean *we?* You're the one who's causing the scene."

Rachel was forced under threat of torture to reveal every tiny detail of the evening. The questioning went on so long that she was late for class. Rushing down the hall, she went right into the lesson without even a glance out the window, so she jumped as a crack of thunder rattled the walls. Peeking out the blinds, she was surprised to find a massive, dark cloud had completely blotted out the sun. The wind howled around the building and lightning popped. Rachel's heart began to beat rapidly, but she turned back to her students and tried to resume the lesson. In a few moments, it became apparent that class was over when the power flickered and the room went dark. There was a general cry from the students.

"It's okay, everybody. It's just the storm. Lightning probably hit the transformer or something. Hold on just a minute." Rachel dug in her "portable office" and found a flashlight. Her students sighed in relief when she flipped it on. "Just to be sure, let's go downstairs to the basement until the storm passes."

There was a general murmur of gibberish as the women reverted to their native tongues. Rachel looked back to make sure they were all behind her. They looked and sounded like a gaggle of geese waddling down the hall. She started to giggle, but it ended up almost a sob. Rachel wasn't sure how she was going to get them all down the dark staircase. Just then, Susan came out with a handful of candles, some matches, and another flashlight. In moments, the hallway looked like a festival of lights. The women inched downstairs and made their way into a room at the back of the building. There were no windows because one wall was underground and the other was an interior wall.

Susan had just closed the door behind the last student when a hush fell. No more howling or cracks of thunder, just an eerie silence. Rachel's instinct told her what she didn't want to know.

"Everybody. Blow out your candles and get against the wall." The women looked frightened, but did as she asked. Rachel looked around for something, anything, to cover their heads with. A mattress that had just been donated to the Center was standing in the corner. "Susan, help me." Together they pulled the mattress over to the women. Rachel and Susan crawled under the crude tent at each end; at the same instant the fury of the storm resumed. The wind roared like a lion and the building began to shake. Cries were heard over the sound of tearing wood and breaking glass. It lasted only a couple of minutes, but it seemed like an eternity.

The howling subsided, leaving only the rain behind. Crawling out from under the mattress, Rachel turned on her flashlight and began to explore. The basement still seemed intact. Susan remained with the women while Rachel went upstairs. She was not prepared for the sight that waited at the top of the stairs. Where her room once had been, a giant oak tree now resided. Rain was flowing steadily in at every corner. She just stood there for several minutes, staring. It must be an illusion. She reached out and touched a limb. It was very real.

After several stunned moments, Rachel made her way back down the now slippery staircase. The women were huddled near the mattress.

"Is it all clear?" Susan asked.

"You could say that."

"What do you mean?"

"You'll just have to see for yourself. We need to get upstairs, but be careful because the steps are slick." Rachel went first, carrying the flashlight. The other women followed with Susan bringing up the rear. Susan looked at the damage, but nothing came out of her mouth. She was quiet so long that Rachel was beginning to get worried.

"It'll be alright, Susan."

She shook her head. "Of course. Everything will be alright." She sounded like a zombie. She walked around, mumbling, the rain soaking her clothes.

"Come in here, Susan. You're soaked." She obeyed like a child. Rachel had to tell her to take a towel from the storage room and dry off as much of her hair and face as she could. Her students moved like one massive body, arms hooked together, eyes wide with fright.

It was almost thirty minutes before rescue workers made their way into the building. There were trees and power lines down in every direction. Through a policeman, Rachel learned that the university had been spared. There had been sightings of a funnel cloud, but so far this block was the only one with severe damage. The rescue workers took Susan to the hospital. They said she was suffering from shock. Rachel stayed behind until all the women had been checked and released. Then she arranged for a volunteer with a van to take the women home. When everyone was gone, she stood staring at the building from the outside. The oak tree was resting in her classroom. How was she going to teach her students?

"Miss, do you need a ride home?"

"Huh?" Rachel looked to see a man from the power company standing beside her.

"Do you need a ride home? You're soaked to the skin." He pulled a blanket around her shoulders.

"I'm not sure."

"I'll take her home." Rachel felt a hand on her shoulder. She turned to find Dr. Harris. "Come on, Rachel. You took care of everybody else. Now it's time to take care of you." He pulled the blanket tighter and wrapped his arm around her to keep it in place. Then he led her through the maze of debris and fallen trees to his car.

Her apartment was just as she had left it. A few limbs scattered across the lawn was the only sign of a disturbance. Dr. Harris followed her inside, and she didn't argue.

He disappeared into the back while she stood in the middle of the floor, dripping. She heard the sound of water running and then he returned.

"You need to get out of those wet clothes. I took the liberty of starting a hot bath. I put some of the aromatherapy salts in. Why don't you get some dry clothes from your closet while the tub is filling up?"

She went to her bedroom still holding the wet blanket and finally had to drop it so she could get out some clean clothes. Then she went back into the living room, clutching the clothing. He took them out of her hands and carried them to the bathroom for her. She followed like a puppy.

"Randy? How am I going to teach my students?"

"I don't know, Rachel," he said, shaking his head, "but we'll think of something. Go ahead and take your bath. I'll be in the kitchen."

It was oddly comforting to Rachel to know that someone else was here. She sank into the hot, scented water with a sigh. It wasn't until feeling began returning to her hands and feet that she realized how cold she had really been. She stayed in the tub until the water lost its warmth and then she quickly dressed. She found Randy in the kitchen, cooking.

"What are you doing?" she asked.

"Cooking. What does it look like?" he replied.

"That's what I thought. Why?"

"You sure do ask a lot of questions. Why don't you just sit down and enjoy it?"

"Okay," Rachel said with a puzzled look on her face. Taking a seat at the breakfast nook, she watched him neatly fold an omelet. "I've never been able to do that."

"It's all in the wrist. I'll show you sometime." He slid it onto a plate and then cut it in half, sliding the second half onto another plate. "I hope you don't mind sharing. You're a little short on ingredients," he said, motioning toward the almost empty cabinet.

"I haven't been to the grocery store yet."

"So I see."

They ate dinner in comfortable silence, and he stayed long enough to clean up the dishes. "If you need anything, just call me. I left my home number on the fridge. Okay?" She nodded her head in agreement.

"See you tomorrow?" she said. It was more a question than a statement.

"Yeah," he replied and then disappeared behind the door.

She locked the door behind him, and a sudden weariness flooded her body. She turned off the lights and stumbled to the bed, exhaustion claiming her before her head hit the pillow.

# five

The telephone rang early the next morning, waking Rachel from a sound sleep. She reached for the alarm, and realizing her mistake, grabbed the receiver. She heard, more than felt, her Bible fall off the nightstand. "Hello?" she whispered.

"Rachel? Are you all right?"

"Mama?" Rachel sat up quickly—too quickly. She sank back against the pillows.

"Of course, it's me. Are you all right?" Anxiety was evident in the way she talked through her teeth. When her mother was anxious, she often appeared angry. It was something Rachel had come to recognize.

"I'm fine."

"You sound horrible," Edna Grant replied. As usual, her words of concern sounded more like an insult.

"Of course, I sound horrible. You woke me out of a sound sleep. Do you have any idea what time it is?" Rachel replied. Once again her mother had her all defensive, and all she had done was express concern. What was it with the two of them?

"It's a quarter past six. You're usually up and getting ready for class by now."

Feeling guilty for her outburst, Rachel tried again. "I

know, I just got to bed late, that's all."

"That's why I'm calling. I heard about the community center. They said there were no injuries, but I wanted to call and make sure. I tried your apartment several times last night, but there was no answer. I was beginning to get worried."

"I'm fine. It just took a while to get all the students home and for the power company to clean up the power lines." The scene replayed through her mind like a movie. She could almost see the tree resting on her classroom table. She shook away the image as her mother's voice broke into her thoughts.

"Rachel, are you still there?"

"Yes, Mama. I was just thinking. I'm still a little groggy. Can we talk later?"

"All right," her mother said with a sigh. "Just make sure you call me back. Better than that, why don't you just come home this weekend?"

Rachel hesitated. There was so much that needed to be done.

"It's been three months since you've been home to visit. With the Center closed for now, you should have some extra time on your hands. There's nothing going on that can't wait over the weekend," her mother cajoled.

"Okay. I'll come down late Friday."

"Good. I'll see you then." The phone went dead before Rachel could even say good-bye. She stared at the phone in her hand until the dial tone started buzzing. The conversation was always over as soon as Mama got what she wanted. Rachel curled up with a sigh at the prospect of going home. Things never changed, especially not Mama. Since her father's death six years ago, her mother had tried to control her life. After she graduated from college, her mother's one aim was to see Rachel married no matter what. Rachel knew it was only because she cared, but it often seemed her mother thought her incapable of finding a relationship on her own. It wasn't that Rachel was against marriage; she just wanted it to be with the right man, a godly man. Those were few and far between these days.

She didn't have long to think about her family problems because the phone was ringing again. With a groan, she picked it up.

"Girl, what have you been doing on the phone at this hour?" Susan asked.

"It wasn't my idea."

"Somebody got up on the wrong side of the bed this morning."

"I haven't gotten up yet."

"Oh! Sorry." Somehow Susan didn't sound sorry. "I just got some news, and I knew you would want to hear it first thing."

"What now?"

"The Center has been condemned. They want to have it demolished by summer. That's only six weeks away!" The stress was evident in Susan's voice.

"Already? The damage just happened last night!" Rachel struggled up in bed and plumped the pillow behind her. "How could they make the decision so fast?"

"It seems the committee had a meeting about this last week. The tornado damage was just the clincher. What are we going to do, Rach?"

"I don't know." Rachel struggled for an answer, but her mind was a jumble of images and voices. It was too much, too fast. "I don't know. We'll think of something." Her words sounded hollow to her own ears, and she knew she wasn't fooling Susan either.

"Yeah. Right. We'll think of something."

"I'll meet you down at the Center after class, okay?" Rachel asked.

"Sure. I'll talk to you later."

Rachel hung up the phone and sank against the pillows like a lead weight. Her body felt too heavy to move. What about her students? They would have nowhere to go to study. Most of them were getting ready to apply for citizenship and desperately needed the practice. Not to mention the neighborhood kids who depended on the Center as a place to get away from their family problems. The more she thought about it, the more depressed she became. It took pure willpower to get herself out of bed and into the shower. She still had a job at the university, and she couldn't afford to louse it up.

All the way to the university her mind pondered the situation, but there still seemed no way out. By the time she reached the campus, tears had formed. She pushed them back and took a deep breath. This was no time to get emotional. She had a class to teach.

Rachel took the long way to her class, hoping to avoid Dr. Harris's office. It was going to be hard enough to hide this from her students. She just couldn't face him today as well. She was so engrossed in her thoughts that she wasn't paying attention to where she was going. The impact brought her mind to the present, as a strong arm caught and pulled her close. She was standing nose to nose with Randy Harris. It was several moments before she could catch her breath.

"We meet again," Randy said. He seemed a bit out of breath.

"Oh." Rachel couldn't think of anything to say, so she stood there with her mouth half open, willing her brain to work.

"Are you all right?" Randy's brow wrinkled as if in concern. "Come into my office and sit down for a few minutes."

Despite her protests, he propelled her toward his office, one arm still tight around her waist. Closing the door behind them, he pushed her into his chair and pulled up another for himself. With one hand on either arm of the chair, he looked closely at her. She lowered her eyes and tried to avoid his gaze, but he wasn't giving up.

"What's the matter, Rachel?" He put a finger under her chin and lifted her face to his.

"Nothing. It just scared me a little when I bumped into you. I wasn't paying attention to where I was going. I'll be fine," she assured him.

"I don't think so. What's really bothering you?" He stared at her with such concern in his eyes that her resolve melted and the tears that had been so close to the surface all morning finally made their way down her cheeks. "Hey, hey. It's okay." He pulled her over to the loveseat against the wall and stroked her hair. She laid her head on his shoulder and cried until her body shook with sobs. He just held her, stroking her hair and whispering comforting words. After a few minutes, the tears stopped and she jumped and looked at his watch.

"What time is it?" she cried.

"Eight o'clock. Why?"

"I have class. I have to go or I'll be late." She started to get up, but he held her firmly in place.

"I don't think so."

"I don't have any choice." She tugged at his arm even though, inside, the last thing she wanted to do right now was teach a class. "Let me go. I have to get to class."

"Not today. You need a break, especially after yesterday. I'll call the office and tell them to send someone to notify the class." She spouted incoherent protests, but he ignored her. One arm securing her to his side, he used his free arm to dial the office.

"Why did you do that?"

"You need a break. You won't be any good to the students like this. They'll enjoy the vacation. Besides, it's not like you take off every week. As far as I know, this is the first time you've ever missed class. So relax!"

"I guess you're right." She sank back onto the couch

and realized Randy's arm was still around her. It felt good.

"I know I am. Now why don't you go home and take a nap or go for a walk or something? Just clear your mind for a while."

"Maybe I will."

"Good girl!" He patted her arm. "I'd go with you, but I'm giving a test in a few minutes. You go on and I'll meet you on the quad for lunch."

"I think I'll pass on lunch. I'll just grab something at the apartment." She saw the disappointment in his eyes and she looked away. She needed some time to think.

"Sure. Maybe later."

"Bye," she said as she walked out the door.

❧

Randy watched from his window as she crossed the lawn. There was something she wasn't telling him. He was sure of it. Thinking back to last night, he remembered that stab of fear he felt when he heard the weather report. There was no planning, no thinking it through, just an urgent need to find her. When he heard that the tornado had hit the community center, he knew that Rachel was there and needed him. It had taken almost an hour to get through the rubble to where she was. She had been standing alone looking at the damage, obviously in a state of shock. It had been instinct that made him cross the lawn and take her in his arms. She had followed his instructions meekly, accepting his help as if it were as natural as breathing. Then she had said,

"Randy, what am I going to do?" She had finally called him Randy. It had come out so easily, as though she had been saying it for years. He had wanted to hold her in his arms, but he was afraid he would scare her. And today he had surprised himself too. Maybe he had come on too strong and that was the reason she had suddenly shied away. Maybe. Still, there was something else going on and he was bound and determined to find out what it was.

❧

Rachel walked across campus, but this time she wasn't feeling sorry for herself. It was time to take some action. She reviewed her resources again and mentally went through a list of options. There had to be a way to keep the Center. There just had to be. With that in mind, she turned her steps toward Susan's house.

❧

"I don't see how it could work, Rachel," Susan said for the third time. "There's no funding available for another building. The only reason we had the Center is because the property was donated. There never was any money budgeted for a building. That's why it was in such bad shape."

"But isn't there someone who's willing to let us have classes in an office building or library somewhere? Maybe on campus?"

"That could be a possibility, but that's only short-term. What are we going to do after these classes are finished?"

"I don't know, Susan, but I'm not going to give up without a fight. We owe it to the students to at least finish the term. That will buy us some time to figure out a long-range plan."

"Okay. Okay. I give in." Susan threw her hands up in surrender. "We'll do it your way. You just don't give up, do you?"

"Not when I believe in something. This town needs that Center, whether it knows it or not. There's so much more that we could be doing."

"Whoa there. One thing at a time. First, we find a place to hold classes, and then we conquer the world."

"I'll talk to the university first thing in the morning," Rachel offered.

"Great. I'll see if the church will let us use the basketball court and the fellowship hall for the kids' programs. I'll meet you here tomorrow and compare notes."

"Perfect. Tomorrow we fight."

# *six*

"I can't believe this," Rachel fumed. "Nothing's going the way I planned it!"

"Well, you know what Burns said, 'The best-laid plans of mice and men oft go astray,'" Susan said.

Rachel frowned in reply. Neither the church nor the university were able—or willing—to help. She had spent all morning trying to convince the university to let them use a classroom for the English class. Unfortunately, all the classrooms were either in use or being repaired. The university had just begun an extensive remodeling project hosted by the local chapter of the historical society. She made two rounds of the carpet and was starting a third when she stopped midstride. "That's it!"

"What's it?" Susan stared at her as if she had completely lost it.

"The historical society."

"You lost me. What *are* you talking about?" She emphasized the "are" with decided sarcasm.

"That's our way out of this mess."

"I'm still lost. Can you give me a clue?" Susan rolled her eyes and stuck out her chin as she spoke, her eyebrows furrowed in a question mark.

"Okay. I'll say this slowly so you'll understand. If we can get the historical society to declare the community center a historical landmark, then they can't destroy it and we can get funds to renovate."

"Are you serious? Do you really think that they'll do that?" Susan's eyes popped open with the first hint of hope she had shown since the night of the tornado.

"Yes!" Rachel squealed. "Remember when I went out with Randy?" Susan nodded, so Rachel continued, "Well, we went to a presentation on local historical landmarks. I remember the speaker talking about how the community center used to be a. . ."

"A what?"

"I can't remember, but it was important. Randy will know. I'll call him tonight and ask."

"Great. Now what do we do?"

"I'm not sure, but Randy can help us with the next step."

"You like him, don't you?" Susan prodded.

"Of course I like him. He's a nice guy." Rachel didn't like where this was going.

"I mean you really like him." Susan sat up straight in her chair. "Come to think of it, you haven't mentioned Kyle in a week."

Susan's obvious excitement over her love life made Rachel squirm. "I'm just taking your advice and letting Kyle suffer."

"Oh, forget Kyle! Randy's got a lot more going for him than Kyle."

"How do you know?" Rachel asked. "You haven't even met Randy."

"No, but I've heard you talk about him and I've seen the way you look when you talk about him."

"You're crazy. He's just a friend. A colleague. I'm biding my time until Kyle realizes what he's missing." From the look on Susan's face, she must have made her point.

"Girl, I hope you don't go and mess up a good thing. Randy's the best thing that's happened to you in a long time. Don't throw it away over something you've dreamed up in your imagination."

"I don't know what you're talking about." Rachel put on her best blank look. It didn't work.

"Yes, you do." Susan picked up her bag. At the door she turned back. "Be careful, Rachel."

As the door closed, Rachel breathed a sigh of relief. Susan didn't understand about Kyle, or Randy, for that matter. Pretty soon Kyle would come to his senses. *But what about Randy?* a little voice whispered. What about Randy? He wasn't interested in dating her. They were just friends. Right?

❧

Rachel didn't talk to Randy that night or the next. In her worry about the Center closing, she had forgotten all about midterms, so she spent the evening making out the tests and the next day grading them. Essay papers took such a long time. When it came down to it, the teacher had more work to do than the students, though the students would never agree. With a sigh she put the last grade in her gradebook and glanced at her watch. She had just enough time to freshen up before Bible study.

She breezed past Kyle, abandoning her usual spot for a seat up front. She ignored him completely, not even turning to give him a glance. It was easier than she had thought it would be, especially after the pastor's first words.

"You know Burns said that 'the best laid plans of mice and men oft go astray,' and there's a lot of truth in that statement." It struck Rachel that Susan had said the exact same thing just a few days ago. Her ears pricked up as the pastor continued, "We often make our own plans without really considering what God wants. God has a plan and a purpose for our lives, but if we never stop and ask Him, we'll never know His perfect plan for our lives." The pastor continued, but that last thought kept going round and round in her mind. She tried to dismiss it, shake it off, yet it lingered. She had been so preoccupied that after the service she had walked out without even a word or a look at Kyle. Actually, she wanted to get home and call Randy about the Center. She hurried toward the car with an anticipation about the call that she was unwilling to acknowledge.

Randy answered on the second ring. "Hello?"

"Hi, Randy. It's me. Rachel."

"Hi." His voice warmed considerably at the sound of her voice. "What can I do for you?"

"I need some help. I think I have a way to keep the Center open, but I'm not sure how to go about it."

"Okay. Let's hear it."

"I want to have the community center declared a historical monument, or whatever they call it. I just don't know how to go about doing that. Do you think it will work?"

"Well. . .maybe." His voice gained enthusiasm. "Hey, maybe you've got something there."

"Yeah. Remember that night we went to that presentation? The speaker talked about the Center, but I can't remember now exactly what he said. Do you?"

"Not off the top of my head, but I know how to find out."

"Great! What do I need to do?"

"Why don't you meet me tomorrow for lunch, my treat?" At her hesitation, he added, "It'll give me a chance to make up for canceling your class the other day."

"There's nothing to make up for. You were just being a friend."

"Well, I didn't mean to be so pushy. What do you say? Noon, at our favorite table?" She couldn't miss the anticipation in his tone.

"Okay."

"See you then." As she replaced the receiver, she couldn't help smiling at his reference to "our" table.

❧

Randy hung up the phone and nearly whooped in

delight. With a sudden burst of energy, he headed for the front parlor with his tool belt. He might just have enough time to finish hanging the wallpaper before midnight.

# seven

Rachel had barely replaced the receiver when the phone rang. She jumped in surprise at the sound. It was so rare in her apartment. Before picking it up, she took a deep breath to steady her pulse, but it was a wasted effort. "Hello."

"Hi. Rachel?" a male voice questioned.

"Yes."

"This is Kyle." Those three words sent her pulse skyrocketing. Her mind drew a complete blank. There was a silent pause before he continued. "What's up?"

"Nothing much." That calm-sounding voice couldn't belong to her. "How about you?"

"Not a lot." Silence.

"What can I do for you?" she questioned. More silence.

"Well, you just left so quick tonight that I didn't get a chance to talk to you. We haven't seen much of you lately."

She smiled at the "we." The plan was working. Just stay calm. "I've been busy lately with all the problems at the Center and midterms."

"Yeah. I heard about the Center. It's too bad they're going to tear it down."

"Well, I wouldn't count us out yet. We still have a few

aces up our sleeve."

"That's great." The pause was even longer this time, but she was determined to make him work for it. "Uhmmm. I was wondering if you'd like to go out to lunch tomorrow or something." She finally had him. Every part of her being wanted to scream, "Yes!", but she remembered that she already had plans and she couldn't be rude to Randy.

"I'm sorry, Kyle. I already have a date for tomorrow."

"Oh." That was all and then empty air. "With Susan?" he asked hopefully.

"No. I'm going to lunch with Randy Harris." She could feel him squirming over the line. It was getting to him.

"Who's he?" She detected a note of jealousy.

"He used to be one of my professors, but now we work together at the university."

"A professor."

"Hmm hmm." She tried hard not to giggle at his obvious discomfort.

"Oh. How about dinner?"

"I think I might be free. I'll have to check my datebook. Hold on just a moment." She put her hand over the mouthpiece and gave a silent scream and a little victory dance before returning the phone to her ear. "Sure, Kyle. I'm free tomorrow night."

"Great." He sounded considerably brighter. "I'll pick you up around seven o'clock."

"Sounds good. See you then."

She hung up the phone and screamed for real. She

danced around the room with a smile big enough to light up Central Park. The idea that her dream was finally coming true seemed unreal. Rachel ran back to the phone and dialed Susan's number. Susan had barely said hello before Rachel squealed into the phone.

"Girl, what is wrong with you?" Susan asked.

"Susan it's what's right with me. You're never going to believe what happened. Never in a million years."

"Then save me the trouble and tell me."

"I just got a phone call."

"From Randy?" Susan sounded more interested.

"No. From Kyle."

"Oh. What did he want?" She sounded disappointed.

"He asked me out to lunch, only I already have a date with Randy. You should've heard him. He was so shocked that he didn't know what to say."

"You turned him down," Susan squealed. "You go, girl. Let him eat his heart out."

"But that's not all."

"Spill it. I want to hear it all." She could almost see Susan sitting on the edge of her chair.

"He asked me about Randy and he sounded jealous."

"Good. It's about time somebody showed him a thing or two. Take some of the air out of his balloon."

"Then he asked me out for dinner."

"And you turned him down, right?" Susan hesitated. "You did turn him down, didn't you?" Rachel's silence said more than words. "You said yes," Susan fairly screamed.

"Of course, I said yes. I've been waiting for this for years."

"Why?"

"What do you mean, *why?*" Rachel asked, confused by Susan's attitude. "I thought you'd be happy for me."

"Why do you want to go out with Kyle after the way he's treated you? Especially when you could have a guy like Randy who treats you like a queen."

"How can you talk about Randy when you've never even met him?"

"I've heard how you talk about him. That's all I need to know. Besides, I've known Kyle for a long time, and he's not good enough for you."

"How can you say that? He's wonderful. He's a great Christian, a leader, and good looking."

"Yeah, yeah. I've heard that before. Save it for Kyle."

"I thought you'd be happy for me. I called you as soon as I hung up because I wanted to share my good news, and all you can do is badmouth Kyle."

"I'm sorry, Rachel," Susan relented. "I didn't mean to rain on your parade. I just don't want you to throw away a good thing."

"Let's not go there again. You made your point."

"Okay. Let's talk about something else."

Rachel hung up about ten minutes later. The rest of the conversation had been full of meaningless small talk. Neither of them had felt up to deeper topics. There was a strain in the conversation that made them both feel uneasy. Rachel walked to her room with her heart firmly back in her body and her spirit resting on the floor. She tried to re-create the joy, but it wouldn't come. Something was nagging her about the truth of what Susan had said, but she refused to let it get her down. She dressed for bed and snuggled down with a dream of Kyle and fell asleep with a smile.

# eight

Rachel awoke with a sigh of satisfaction. She had had the most wonderful dream. Kyle had called and asked her out. She popped up out of bed with a bounce. But it wasn't a dream—Kyle had called. They were going out tonight. She was out of bed and ready in record time with even a half hour to spare. Instead of her usual Bible study and quiet time, she painted her nails with wine-glow polish and spent extra time on her hair. Giving one last look in the mirror, Rachel headed for school with more enthusiasm than she had felt in months. She took the stairs with a quick clip and a toss of her hair. Randy noted the change immediately.

"Hey, slow down there. Where's the fire?" Randy asked.

"No fire, unless you consider the spirit capable of being on fire." Rachel's eyes danced and her cheeks couldn't hold back the smile that kept popping up like a jack-in-the-box.

"Well something is definitely different." He waited for a response, but Rachel wasn't sure what to say.

"Let's just say that I had a very good day yesterday and today is looking even better."

"Mysterious, I must say. Don't I even get a hint?"

He was definitely curious now; she could see it in his expression.

"Let me put it this way. God answered a real big prayer last night and I'm really happy about it."

"Okay. Go on. I like the sound of this."

Rachel fought to keep it to herself, but could contain it no longer. "Kyle asked me out for tonight." She saw a hint of something cross Randy's face and then it was gone.

"Who's Kyle?" His voice sounded strained.

"That's funny. He asked the same thing about you. He's a friend of mine from church. I've always felt that God intended for us to be together. I've waited so long for God to open a door, and it finally happened last night."

"Well, I'm happy for you." His face looked strained. *He must be under some kind of pressure,* she thought. Maybe they could talk about it over lunch.

"Are we still on for lunch?" Rachel asked.

"I was just about to go looking for you when you came in, to tell you that I've got a meeting with a student at lunch. Maybe we can do it another time."

"Sure. That'll be fine." She felt oddly disappointed, but then her dinner plans wiped away everything else. "I'll see you later then. I've got class in a few minutes."

"See you later," he mumbled.

Rachel headed for class without even a look over her shoulder. Tonight was going to be great.

❧

Randy heard the words, but they didn't quite sink in until he was seated at his desk. She was going out with some guy named Kyle. She was head over heels for someone else. How could he have been so stupid? He felt as if he were going to be sick, as his stomach tied up into knots and took his breath away. *Lord, did I misunderstand you? It seemed so clear that she was the one, the one I've been waiting for. What went wrong?*

*"Wait on me."*

*Wait on what? Another girl?*

*"Just wait."*

*I don't understand. Why is this happening?* He waited for the still, small voice to answer, but he was met with only silence. He went through the day in a daze, with her words still echoing through the hole in his heart. The house seemed emptier than ever before, and he had no energy to finish the parlor. Wandering from room to room, Randy thought of all the plans he had made. His thoughts strayed to what Rachel was doing right now. The lump in his throat threatened to choke him. He grabbed his tools and headed for the parlor. Anything was better than thinking.

❧

Across town, Rachel was a bundle of nerves. The day had been filled with a series of minor disasters. She had bumbled through classes, trying to hurry so that she would have plenty of time to get ready, only to have students stop her to ask questions. She was thirty minutes later getting home than she had planned. Now she didn't have time to iron the outfit she wanted to wear and redo her hair. She settled on a two-piece pantsuit, then frowned at herself in the mirror. Her light-brown hair was wind blown, and her face was oily. A little make-up took care of the latter, but twenty minutes worth of struggle could not make her hair do anything. Rachel huffed in frustration and then ran her fingers through the medium locks until they settled into the style she normally wore, natural waves and wispy bangs around her face. As she sprayed the last puff of hairspray over her head, the doorbell rang, jump-starting her pulse.

All the way to the door she did deep-breathing exercises, but her heart was still skipping along. She took one last deep breath as she reached for the doorknob. Kyle was as handsome as ever in a dark-green dress shirt that brought out his eyes, and black slacks. He leaned against the door frame and gave her a long look.

"Hi, Kyle."

"Hi." He paused for a moment, still staring at her.

"Is there something wrong?" she asked, looking down for a spot or stain on her outfit.

"No. You look perfect. It's just that I didn't realize how beautiful you really are. I can't believe that I never noticed before."

Rachel could feel her face getting warm. She turned around and reached for her purse with a mumbled thank you. He started to walk around the car without opening the door for her but then at the last minute turned around and got it. Rachel pretended not to notice, but it irked her that he almost had to be reminded. She pushed it out of her mind and tried to concentrate on the evening.

They went to a crowded steak restaurant with loud music. Whenever they talked, she could hardly hear what Kyle was saying. Friends kept coming up to him and talking. Most of the time, he didn't even bother to introduce her. Then, they went to an action movie with a lot of explosions and gunfire. When the movie was over, he took her home and walked her to the door.

"I had a great time tonight, Rachel. Maybe we can do it again sometime."

"Sure, that'd be great."

He smiled that smile and her knees went soft. She leaned against the door frame for support. He leaned in and kissed her softly, and then bounded down the steps with a quiet good-bye. Rachel watched until the car lights disappeared, and then stumbled into the house.

Getting ready for bed, Rachel thought back over the evening. Somehow it just wasn't what she had expected. It was like the prom. She got all excited and dressed up, and it was nothing special, kind of a letdown. They hadn't talked very much, and steak wasn't her favorite food. But there was the kiss. She smiled at the memory. Things would go better when they got used to each other. He was probably just nervous because it was their first date. With that settled in her mind, she went to bed.

# nine

The date with Kyle had left her feeling let down, and thoughts of going home for the weekend had not raised her spirits in the least. By lunch on Friday, Rachel was dragging. Everything about her slouched. She dawdled in her classroom as long as she could, but she knew that it was time to hit the road. Maybe she would have a flat tire, or a dead battery, or maybe a truck would run over her on the way out of town. Anything would be acceptable at this point.

"If your bottom lip got any lower, you would be dusting the floor with it."

"Huh?" Rachel's head jerked to attention.

"What's the problem?" Randy asked. At his look of concern, she felt her spirits rise.

"It's just been one of those days," she lied. He nodded his head and then gave her a piercing look. It was as if he could read her mind.

"Why do I get the feeling that you're feeding me a line?"

She averted her eyes until she felt his hand under her chin. He tugged gently until she looked him in the eye. His face was mere inches from her own. She sucked in her breath as their eyes locked and an electric current shot between them. Held them. Connected them. It seemed like hours, but lasted only seconds. Then, he stepped back, and it was gone. She searched for the right words, for any words, but her mind was a white canvas.

"Why don't you come into my office and tell me what's really bothering you?"

"I can't. I promised Mama that I'd be home in time for dinner." He looked disappointed, but he only nodded his head. "When I get back, I want to talk with you about the Center."

"Sure. How about after class on Monday?"

"That'll be great. See you then."

"Yeah. Monday." She gave a weak wave and then turned down the hall. As she turned the corner, she sneaked a look and found him staring after her. Their eyes met again for an instant before she bolted down the stairs.

❧

From Myerstown to Birmingham, Rachel tried to ignore the rerun of that moment in the hall. She tried to erase it from her mind, but, like a bad song that got stuck in her head, it kept going around and around. She tried to focus on Kyle, but that only brought up other issues. She wished she could just shut off her brain for a few hours. But the minute she pulled into the drive, she knew that any hope of peace was gone.

"It's about time you got here, Rachel. We were worried sick."

"Who's 'we'?" Rachel asked.

"Why, Dale, of course. He's been here almost half an

hour, waiting on you."

Rachel's heart sank like a fifty-pound weight. "What's Dale doing here?" she said through clenched teeth.

"He came to see you," Edna replied.

"How did he know I was coming, Mama?"

"I called him and invited him to dinner the minute I knew you were coming home. I knew he would want to see you, and I was sure you would feel the same way." Edna put her hands on her hips and lowered her voice. "I just don't understand you. Dale is a nice, young man, and you just tossed him aside like garbage."

Rachel raised her hands. "Mama, I don't want to talk about it. Let's just go in and get this over with."

"Get this over with. Get this over with." Edna closed her eyes. "Lord, help me. I just don't understand you."

"That's obvious," Rachel said, half to herself. Still, her mother heard, and Rachel could feel the cold air descending. Nothing had changed.

Dinner was a strained affair filled with her mother's incessant chatter about nothing. The tension was obviously getting to her. Rachel refused to help her in any way, shape, or form. This was Mama's own doing. She would have to live with the consequences. Rachel thought she was in the clear about where she stood until time for dessert.

"Well, Rachel, we'd better get a move on if we're going to beat the weekend crowd," Dale said. He wiped his mouth one more time, and then laid his napkin neatly on the table.

"Excuse me?" Rachel said.

"I told Dale that I didn't need any dessert. I'm watching my figure, you know. I asked him if he wouldn't mind taking you out for dessert." Edna Grant put on her sweetest, most innocent smile.

Rachel looked from one to the other. It was a conspiracy. They were in on this together. Well, it wasn't going to work this time. They weren't going to shame her into doing something she didn't want to do.

"I'm afraid I'm on a diet myself. Too much sugar is bad for you." Rachel smiled sweetly while inside she burned with indignation.

"A little bit won't hurt. Someone as pretty as you doesn't need to worry about one little dessert," Dale replied. His sugared words melted in the fire in her eyes. He realized too late that he had taken the wrong tactic.

"Actually, I've been looking forward to spending time with Mama. I haven't seen her in three months. So, if you don't mind, I'll have to bow out this time. Why don't you go ahead? I'm sure there are plenty of people at McKnight's to keep you company."

Dale's face colored slightly, but he had the good sense to take the hint. Despite her mother's protests to the contrary, Dale left ten minutes later. Rachel sighed as she heard his car pull out of the drive. But her respite was short.

"Rachel Grant! I cannot imagine what just got into you. That was so rude and inconsiderate."

"*I* was rude and inconsiderate? *You're* the one who invited him knowing good and well that I never wanted to see him again."

"Why? He's such a nice, polite young man."

"He's nice to you because he wants you to trust him. That's the way he works, Mama." Rachel pushed her chair away from the table and picked up her plate. Her mother's voice followed her into the kitchen.

"You're just too picky. One day you're gonna find yourself all alone."

"That's enough, Mama!" Rachel's voice took on a sharp edge. "I don't want to talk about this anymore. You obviously will never understand." Rachel put the dishes down with a bang.

"Don't you talk to me that way, young lady. I raised you, and I deserve a little respect."

"So do I, Mama. So do I." Rachel turned on her heel and went back to the dining room. She started stacking the dishes to give herself something to do with her hands. It was either that or strangle Mama.

Moments later, she heard the back door slam and the screech of the screen door as it bounced closed. Rachel continued to clean off the table and load the dishwasher. She scrubbed the counters and appliances until everything glowed. She scrubbed Dale's image from the stove, but she couldn't get their first and only date out of her mind.

At the urging of her mother, she had gone out with Dale six months ago. He seemed charming enough and very attentive. The first part of the date was fine. They went to a movie and dinner. He was a perfect gentleman, opening doors and holding her chair. However, on the way home, he turned into a dead-end street and parked in the shadows.

"Why are we stopping here?"

"I just wanted to spend a little time alone with you," Dale said. He put his arm across the back of the seat, and before she knew what was happening, his open mouth was on hers. She pushed him away, but he kept coming back like an octopus. Finally, Rachel punched him in the jaw, sending him back to his corner.

"What was that for?" he yelled.

"Take me home."

"Fine!" He started the car and slammed it into gear. He must have left half of his tread on the asphalt. They made it home in record time, although he did slow down when he got within a block of her house.

She had never felt comfortable telling her mother about that night, despite the fact that her mother kept asking her about Dale. She had skirted the issue until the weekend was over and then hurried back to her quiet apartment in Myerstown. She thought she had heard the last of him, but some nightmares just kept coming back. What would possess Dale to think she was still interested in him? Why would he still be interested in her after their date? It had to be her mother. Would she ever learn to stop meddling?

An hour later, Edna Grant came in, quiet and sulky.

Rachel waited until she had settled into her seat in the living room before she started.

"Mama, I want you to promise me something."

"What?" she bit out.

"Promise me that you'll never invite that man over here again, especially not in my presence."

"Don't I have the right to invite anyone I want into my home?" Edna sat up straight. "This is still my home, isn't it?"

"Of course it is, Mama, but I don't ever want to see him again. If I ever think you're going to pull something like this again, then I won't come back to visit. Do you understand?" Edna's mouth tightened into a thin line. "Do you understand, Mama?"

"Fine. You can die an old maid if you want to. I wash my hands of the matter." She got up and exited the room with a flourish.

Rachel sighed and turned on the TV. Maybe there was a good movie on.

Her mother never said another word the rest of the weekend, except to ask what she wanted for dinner and to say good-bye. It was with great relief that Rachel got into the car after lunch on Sunday. The minute the house was out of sight, she floored the gas pedal and hightailed it for home.

# ten

Randy spent the weekend finishing the wallpaper in the dining room. All it needed now was some furniture and pictures. He looked around and sighed. What it really needed was a woman's touch. Rachel's face popped into his mind. *What was she doing tonight? What does it matter what she's doing tonight? She made it clear the other day that she was interested in someone else. But what about Friday and that parting look?* The argument went on, back and forth.

He cleaned up the dining room and moved his tools to the master bedroom. It and the bathroom were the only rooms left needing repairs. He had put it off time and again. The bedroom was empty except for his tools and the sawhorses. Empty like the rest of the house. He tried to shake off the dark mood that was descending on his spirit, but it was like trying to shake off a leech. It just hung there and sucked the blood from his veins. He was tired of living alone, tired of the overwhelming silence.

He lifted his eyes toward the ceiling. "What am I doing all this for? If I don't have someone to share it with, then, what's the point?" He waited, but his prayer seemed to have bounced off the roof. The heaviness in his chest felt like a physical weight. He sat on the dusty floor with his head in his hands. Tears flowed unbidden down his cheeks.

*"I'm here."*

"That's not the point. I need someone tangible, human, to talk to and laugh with."

*"I'm here."*

"I know, but I need someone all my own. You gave Eve to Adam because he was lonely. Why can't you do the same for me?"

*"I'm here, Randy. I'm all you need."*

He nodded, then picked himself up. He had gotten his answer, like it or not.

❧

Monday morning, he rushed through grading papers, so that nothing would detain him from his meeting with Rachel. He still had a chance with her. He could sense it in the way she had looked at him Friday. With a flourish of almost unintelligible script, he finished the last paper and threw it on the stack. All he needed now was a rubber band to hold the pages together and he was ready to go.

Rachel came by at the usual time, more subdued than normal. Something was wrong. He wished he could help her, but something told him to wait. A part of him wanted to reach out and pull her into his arms. Still, he held back.

"Hi, Rachel. Have a nice weekend?" The look on her

face told him before she ever opened her mouth.

"No. How about you?" She colored and tried again. "I'm sorry. I didn't mean to sound so. . .so. . ."

"Honest." He smiled, then she laughed.

"Yeah."

"Well, as it happens, I had a lousy weekend myself, so I can empathize. How about we go to lunch and not talk about it."

"Sounds like a plan to me."

❧

Seated in their favorite corner of The Magnolia, Rachel watched as Randy waited at the counter for their order. She wondered if his weekend had gone as badly as hers. He brought the food over and sat down opposite her.

"Now, what did you want to talk about?"

She took a sip of her iced tea. "Well, I'm just not sure what to do about the Center. The university can't help and the city won't help. I asked the church if we could use the fellowship hall, but that's out too. Did you have any luck with the historical society?"

"I called and talked to the local chairperson who said all their funds are tied up right now, but she implied that it wasn't a worthwhile project."

"Wasn't worthwhile!" Rachel's head popped up and her eyes sparked. "What do they mean, not worthwhile? Don't they know what goes on out there? Don't they care?" she sputtered.

"Hey! Don't shoot the messenger." Randy raised

his hands in surrender. "I'm only repeating what they told me."

"I'm sorry, Randy. I didn't mean to yell at you. It's just been a long weekend followed by a Monday."

"I can relate." Randy reached across and covered her hand with his. A shiver ran up her spine. "Hey, you're not cold, are you?"

"No. I'm fine. Just a reflex." She shrugged it off.

"Do you want to talk about this weekend?" He shot her a piercing look, and another shiver threatened to run loose.

"What do you mean?" She took another sip of tea to avoid looking him in the eye.

"Rachel, I can tell something's wrong." He lifted her chin until their eyes met. "Let me help you." She could see the concern in his eyes, such beautiful eyes. Warm brown pools that she could drown in. His hand encircled hers, and she could feel the warmth spreading to her cheeks. She wanted to tell him everything, but something held her back, some unknown fear clamped down on her tongue and robbed her of the words.

"I just had a little fight with my mom. No big deal. I'll be fine." She pulled her hand back, breaking the connection. "So, what do we do about the Center?"

He leaned back in his chair with a sigh. For a moment, she thought he would try again. She held her breath, but he let her change the subject. She felt oddly disappointed. Talk turned back to the Center and their options.

There didn't seem to be any more choices.

"There's only one thing left that I can think of," Randy said with resignation.

"What's that?"

"Prayer."

# eleven

Randy's words echoed through her mind all week. Rachel took his words to heart and began to pray over the situation. She couldn't get the feel of his hand on hers or the look in his eyes out of her mind. She prayed for understanding and guidance. Thursday she flipped open her Bible at random. The words of David from the book of Psalms seemed to jump off the page. "Wait on the Lord." She closed the book with a thud. She didn't have time to wait.

Kyle called for another date on Friday, and again on Saturday. With each date, Rachel became more and more frustrated. They were all the same as the first. They went to the movies or out to eat, but the conversation never got past small talk. More and more, she found herself thinking about her conversations with Randy. In a few meetings, Rachel had learned more about him than she had learned about Kyle in five years. She wanted to talk to Susan about it, but she could already hear the lecture and see the knowing look. She would just have to work this out on her own, or better yet, talk it out with Kyle. Maybe he just needed a little push in the right direction. She picked up the phone and dialed his number.

"Hello." Somehow the sound of his voice was annoying. She shook the thought away.

"Hi, Kyle. It's Rachel. I wanted to talk to you about Friday night." She wound the phone cord around her fingers as she talked.

"What about it? You're still free, aren't you?" The worry in his voice made her smile.

"Yes. It's not that. I was just wondering if we could skip the movie and go somewhere and get to know each other better."

"Oh, sure. That would be good. Where do you want to go?"

"I don't know. Just some place we can talk without so many people around."

"I know just the place. Why don't I surprise you?" Something about the tone in his voice sent a warning shiver up her spine, but she ignored it. It was probably just nerves.

"Okay."

"See you Friday."

She hung up and finished getting ready for work. Monday was the same old thing, a repeat of the Monday before it. She hadn't seen much of Randy since their meeting the week before. It was almost as if he were avoiding her. It was probably just her imagination. He probably had a lot of grading to do. With a sigh, she picked up a one-inch stack of papers and added them to her growing tower of papers.

The rest of the week was a blur of grading and classes.

One day proceeded after another in their onward march to eternity. She was getting overly dramatic these days. What was the problem? She should be happy, ecstatic, but here she was moaning and groaning. She finally had Kyle, so why was she so depressed? She stuffed the stacks of papers into her bag and headed for the Magnolia. Maybe a cappuccino would help.

She spotted him the minute she walked into the room. Randy was sitting in their favorite spot, holding a cup of cappuccino like it was a lifeline. Rachel ordered her coffee and made her way through the tables, her step definitely lighter.

"Hey, stranger! What do you know?"

He jumped at the sound of her voice, spilling hot liquid all over his hand. "Ow!" he yelped. She put down her coffee and grabbed some napkins in one smooth move. She dried his hand and checked for burns. On a whim, she kissed his hand.

"There. I kissed it and made it better."

❧

The scalding coffee was nothing compared to the fire that went through him at the touch of her lips on his hand. He wanted nothing more than to grab her and kiss her right then. Her smile seemed to light up the entire room. It had been a long two weeks without that smile. He had made a concerted effort to stay out of her path, hoping he could shake the growing need to see her. It only brought pain, especially when he thought of the other guy.

"What's wrong?" She looked concerned. "Does it still hurt?" She turned his hand over and inspected it again.

"Oh, it's nothing. I was just surprised, that's all."

"Well, I'm sorry I startled you. Can I buy you another cappuccino to make up for it?" she asked. Everything in him said to get up and leave. Everything except his heart which was crying, "Stay!" His heart won.

"Sure."

They talked about school, the weather, politics. Anything that wasn't personal. They stretched the coffee as long as they could, neither one in a hurry to leave—both unwilling to leave. Finally, he got up.

"Well, I have a meeting in five minutes. I guess I'd better get a move on."

"Oh. Okay." She seemed disappointed. His heart grasped at the hope that there was still a chance.

"Maybe we could have dinner afterwards?" Then she lowered the boom.

"I'm sorry, but I already have a date tonight."

The words cut through him like a knife. He stood in shock while she gathered her things. He struggled to sound normal. "Oh. Well, maybe another time."

"Maybe."

"I'll see you later, then." He turned and walked toward the door, the walking wounded.

# twelve

Randy walked back to his office, shoulders slouched. He tried to shake off the feelings of depression that threatened to overwhelm him. It just wasn't meant to be. God had other plans for him. He would just have to wait on God's timing. He repeated the words to himself over and over again, but nothing loosened the knot growing in his throat. He was so engrossed in his thoughts that he almost didn't see the young man standing in front of his office.

"Excuse me." Randy jumped at the sound of the voice. "Didn't mean to scare you."

"I should of been paying more attention," Randy replied with a shrug of his shoulders. "What can I do for you?"

"I'm looking for Rachel Grant. Have you seen her?"

"Yes. I just left her at The Magnolia."

"Yeah?" Kyle looked Randy over with a suspicious eye. "What were you doing there?"

"Having a cappuccino, if it's any business of yours." Randy straightened to his full six feet, but this guy was still a head taller. He didn't like this guy's tone of voice, but he didn't want to start anything in the hallway.

"Well, if you were having it with my fiancée, then it

is my business," Kyle said, his lip turning into smirk.

"Fiancée?" Randy couldn't have heard right.

"Yeah, that's right. It's not official or anything, but it's understood." Kyle leaned against the wall, obviously enjoying himself.

"Rachel never said anything about an engagement." Randy felt his heart drop, but he had his doubts about this character.

"She probably didn't want to make a big deal out of it. We'll wait until I buy her a ring before we make any announcements." Kyle stood up and pointed toward the quad. "Is The Magnolia out there?" Randy gave a weak nod. "Then, I guess I'd better get going before I miss her." Kyle sauntered down the hall with a backward wave. "See you around, Professor."

Randy blindly searched for the right key to his office. Stumbling into his office, he closed and locked the door behind him before sinking into his chair. He raked his fingers through his hair. He felt like he was going to be sick. Could it be true? Had Rachel already made her choice? If it was true, why hadn't she said anything? He moaned into his hands. How had he let it go this far? Deep in his heart he knew he loved Rachel. How could he stay here, seeing her every day, knowing she belonged to someone else? Worse still, what if she moved away? How could he stay here even if she left? Everything at Myerstown reminded him of Rachel.

He tried to pray, but the words wouldn't come. Finally, he took a deep breath, smoothed his hair and suit, and gathered the papers he needed for the faculty meeting. A few minutes later he was sitting in the conference room pretending nothing was happening, while inside everything was crumbling to pieces.

Dr. Jenson, the president of the university, stood and called the meeting to order. "I called this meeting to tell those of you with tenure about our plans to open a satellite school in Dothan which will offer courses for military personnel at the local Air Force base. There will be openings for several full-time instructors, as well as a position for an administrator. We would like to hire local people for the main teaching positions, but we want the administrator to be someone from this school who is willing to move. It will be a promotion and a significant pay raise." Randy barely heard the rest of the information. It was like a lifeline being thrown to a drowning man. Surely this was God at work, giving him a way out of his suffering. He latched onto the idea like a lifejacket.

As soon as the meeting was over, Randy singled out Dr. Jenson about the job. When he left thirty minutes later, he felt confident that he had a good chance of getting the job. Of course, he would have to apply like anyone else, but he had all the qualifications and was young and unattached, which made moving that much easier. He would know for sure in a couple of weeks.

Driving home, Randy found himself going through Rachel's neighborhood. On impulse he stopped in front of her house. He turned off the engine and looked up at her apartment. He could see her silhouette in the window. He needed to talk to her one more time, make sure before he made his final decision. With a slap to the steering wheel, he got out of the car and started up to her door.

❧

Rachel paced around the room, looking at her watch every thirty seconds. She tried a few deep breaths to control her nerves, but nothing seemed to help. She just had to face it. She did not like confrontations of any kind. Yet, she just couldn't go on this way with Kyle.

Something had to give or change. She wanted a deeper, more intimate relationship than what they had, or she wanted out. Rachel stopped midpace at the realization that had just hit her. All this time she had wanted nothing more than for Kyle to notice her, and now that he had, she wasn't happy. Why?

The doorbell rang, interrupting her thoughts. She opened it without looking in the peephole. "Hi, Kyle. . ." Kyle's name died on her lips as she looked into Randy's eyes. She stood there for a moment, mouth open. Gathering herself together, she clamped her mouth shut. "What are you doing here?"

"I'm not sure." They stood looking at each other in the doorway for several minutes.

"May I come in?" Randy asked.

"No. Yes. I mean, I'm expecting someone."

"I know, but this won't take long."

"Okay." She stepped back for him to enter. She glanced

down the street before she closed the door. No sign of Kyle.

She watched Randy pace around the room. Something was obviously on his mind. "Randy, is something wrong? You look upset."

"Nothing's wrong. I just needed to talk to you about a decision I need to make. I wanted your input." He raked his fingers through his hair. A part of her wanted to repeat the gesture.

"What is it?"

"I just found out about a job opportunity in Dothan. It would be an administrative position, more money. I have a good chance at getting the job, but I'm not sure if it's a good idea or not. What do you think?" He gave her one of his piercing looks.

"I'm not sure. It sounds like a great opportunity." Rachel turned so that he couldn't see her face. She knew it probably reflected the sudden pain she felt in her chest. She didn't want to lose him. A good friend was hard to find. She ignored the little voice that questioned, *Just a friend?*

"Can you think of any reason why I shouldn't take the job? Anything that could keep me in this area?"

She could feel his eyes watching her every move. What did he want? Her approval. "I don't know, Randy. I think that has to be up to you." She gathered up her courage and faced him. "I mean we've become good friends and. . ." The doorbell interrupted her mid-sentence. She opened the door to find Kyle lounging in the doorway. One look at the professor and he pulled himself up.

"What's going on here?" Kyle asked. "I thought we had a date for tonight." Rachel didn't like his tone at all.

"Randy needed some advice. We were just talking about a possible job opportunity."

"Really. What kind of opportunity?" Kyle demanded.

"An administrative job in Dothan," Randy replied.

"Sounds like a good thing to me," Kyle said.

"Well, I'd better be going, Rachel. You two have plans, I'm sure." Randy nodded at both of them and slipped out the door, leaving Rachel feeling torn and awkward. She wanted tell him that they should talk about it later, but he was already halfway down the walk.

"Come on, Rachel. Let's go. I've got a surprise for you."

# thirteen

In the car, Rachel silently fumed. The more she thought about it, the more Kyle's attitude made her just plain mad. How dare he strut around, acting as if he owned her?

She was so lost in her anger that she didn't notice where they were headed until they stopped on a remote road that led to the old drive-in theater. The drive-in had been closed so long that the original name had long since been forgotten—now it was simply called "Lovers' Lane." Rachel looked around in confusion. What were they doing here? She was just about to ask Kyle when the words were blocked by his lips. She pushed at his chest, but he used the momentum to get one arm around her while the other was moving into forbidden territory. The weight of his body pushed her back into the seat and suddenly the car seemed to move. Then she realized that somehow he had reclined the seat and he was on top of her, suffocating her. It took a moment for her to realize what was going on, and then her reflexes kicked in, literally. One swift move and he was back in his seat with a howl.

"What was that for?" he yelped. He was bent over double and his face was red with pain and anger.

Rachel had already sat up and was resetting the chair with a snap. "I could ask the same question. What do you think you were doing?" Rachel yelled, her eyes blazing.

"Just what you asked for," he said. He shifted to ease the pain.

"What do you mean?" she asked.

"You said you wanted to get to know each other better. You said we didn't spend enough time alone. What was I supposed to think?"

"That I meant exactly what I said. I wanted to get to know you as a person, not in the biblical sense." Rachel straightened her sweater where roving hands had rumpled it. "I thought you were a Christian." It was more an accusation than a question.

"I am. I go to church every Sunday and Wednesday. I'm a good guy. I don't drink or do drugs." He had recovered enough from the pain to sit up, but he refused to look at Rachel.

"From what just happened, I'd say this wasn't your first time to 'Lovers' Lane,' was it?"

"Well, it's not like I come here every Friday night with a different girl."

"One girl is one too many." Rachel stared at Kyle and wondered how she could be so wrong about a guy. This was not the guy she thought she knew. He was an alien. "This kind of thing can get you into trouble. What if you got carried away?"

Kyle shifted uneasily in his seat. A horrible premonition sent a shiver through her spine. She willed him to tell her it wasn't true, but his silence said more than she wanted to hear. Rachel shook her head slowly, trying to erase the ugly thoughts in her head. He must have known what she was thinking because he immediately began to give excuses.

"Look, Rachel. It's not the same for girls as it is for guys. I'm thirty years old. That's a long time to wait. So, I slipped once or twice. Big deal! Everybody does it."

Rachel's mouth dropped open and then snapped shut. "Everybody doesn't do it, Kyle. Sex is meant for a husband and wife and no one else. All that stuff about it being different for men is just a line, and it's no excuse. And what about the women you slept with, Kyle? What about them? If girls are supposed to stay pure, what about them? Are only certain girls supposed to stay pure, and the rest are free game?"

Kyle didn't answer. He just stared into the night. He had obviously tuned her out. She swallowed the rest of the arguments like a horse pill. Nothing she said would get to him now because he didn't want to admit he was wrong. He had convinced himself that he was in the right.

"Take me home."

Without another word he started the engine and backed out. The ten-minute drive to her apartment seemed like an eternity. She got out of the car without a word and started toward the door. She heard the tires squeal as he pulled away. Nothing would ever be the same again.

Rachel tossed and turned all night, reliving the scene in the car. How could she have been so wrong? How could he sit in church every Sunday without ever being convicted of what he had done? Was it really that different for guys? Was it too much to ask for a guy that waited for marriage? Were they all like Kyle?

The questions went around and around in her head until she was dizzy. Burying her head under her pillow, she tried to drown out the sounds, but it wasn't until the early morning hours that she drifted off into a troubled sleep.

The next morning over coffee, she remembered Randy's visit. The grogginess wore off instantly. A panic seemed to spread through her at the thought of him leaving. What was she going to do? Rachel was taken aback by how much the thought of him leaving upset her. It was almost as upsetting as last night's revelations about Kyle. She mentally shook off the thoughts and tried to concentrate on a plan of action. It didn't matter why she didn't want him to leave—what mattered was how to make him stay. She chewed absently on her fingernail until her cup of coffee was cold, and still no ideas came. Maybe a brisk walk would clear her thoughts.

❧

Randy shifted through the samples of wallpaper and paint again. If he was going to move, he had to finish this house and put it on the market. The master bedroom and bath were the only two rooms left that needed remodeling. He just couldn't decide how he wanted to finish the room. He rubbed his eyes with the back of his hand to relieve the strain. He had been up late last night looking at samples to keep from thinking about Rachel and that Kyle guy. What did she see in him anyway? He pushed the samples away in frustration and got up. Grabbing his coat from the banister where he'd left it the night before, Randy headed for the park.

Whenever he was restless, which seemed to be all the time these days, he headed for the park. A brisk walk always seemed to soothe him and helped him open up his heart to God. He had to get quiet to hear that still, small voice. He walked around the park three times at a quick pace, but he couldn't hear the voice, and the restlessness was still there. He was about to turn around and go home when he spotted Rachel standing in front of the remains of the community center. She was reading a sign. He couldn't tell what it said from this distance, but from the way her shoulders drooped it couldn't be good. He crossed the space between them in a few strides and tapped her shoulder. She whirled around, one hand at her throat.

"Oh, Randy. It's just you. You scared me half to death."

"I'm sorry," he apologized. "I didn't mean to scare you. What's so engrossing that you can't hear footsteps?"

"Read it for yourself." It was a notice of demolition to be completed in less than a week. "What are we going to do?" She looked at him, pleading with him to give her the answer she needed. More than anything, he wished he could help her, but he was fresh out of ideas.

"I honestly don't know, Rachel. Maybe there's nothing we can do."

"But what about my students?"

"What about them? What are they doing now?"

"I'm not sure. I've been so busy trying to save the building that I haven't kept in touch." As she stood thinking, the wind blew her hair around her face. His hand itched to push the wayward strand behind her ear, to run his fingers through the length of it, to kiss the frown from her lips. Just then, she looked up and they were connected for one moment by an unseen force. It lasted only a moment before she turned away. He cleared his throat.

"Maybe you should talk to your students and see what they need. Maybe they don't need this building at all."

She looked at him, and he could see the spark again in her eyes. "It's a place to start anyway. I'm not doing any good standing out here."

"Me either. I guess I should get back to work." She nodded and headed back toward her apartment. She had only gone a few yards before she turned back.

"Randy!" She paused. "Thanks." She gave a little wave and then took off at a run. He gave a halfhearted wave and whispered, "You're welcome." Then he headed back to the samples. He seemed to remember a paint sample the color of the sky on an autumn day. Just like Rachel's eyes.

# fourteen

Rachel hung up the phone and stared at the receiver. That was call number ten and it was all the same. Every student she contacted was involved in other activities, either at church or at the library. None of them seemed upset or distressed by the closing of the Center. Of course, they all thanked her for her help, but they didn't seem lost without her. Rachel continued to stare at the receiver for several more minutes. The ringing of the phone shook her out of her reverie.

"Hello."

"Hi, dear." Rachel almost groaned aloud when she recognized the voice. She just couldn't handle this right now.

"Hi, Mom," Rachel replied. "What's up?"

"Does anything have to be up for me to call my only child?" Her mother's voice took on that martyr's tone Rachel knew so well.

"No, Mother," Rachel said with a sigh. "I just figured you had a reason for calling, that's all."

"I just wanted to check and see how you were getting along since the tornado. Is everything okay at work?" To give her a little credit she did sound concerned. Rachel twisted the phone cord around her finger.

"I'm fine. They're going to demolish the Center, but my students all seem okay with it. I don't know what Susan's going to do, but I'm sure she'll find another job."

"Of course she will. She's a smart girl." Her mother sounded cheerful, but a little stiff, as if she was forcing the words out.

"Mother, is there something in particular you wanted to talk about?"

"Well, yes, but I don't want to start fighting again." Rachel tightened the cord around her fingers, waiting for the punch line. "I gave Dale your address. Now, don't start yelling. He wants to apologize, to make it up to you for last time. Why don't you give him another chance?"

Rachel could feel the cord cutting off her circulation. "I gave him another chance, Mama. He blew it. I don't ever want to see him again."

"Why not?" Her mother's voice shrilled over the line. Rachel held the phone a few inches away from her face. "He's a nice young man and he's interested in you." Rachel felt her muscles clench. The way she said it made it sound as if she were lucky to have anyone interested at all.

"What do you think, Mother? Do you think I'm desperate? That I should take the first thing that comes along and be grateful?" Rachel could feel the tears and anger rising in her throat, making her voice hoarse.

"No, but you can't be so picky. You're not getting any younger, you know. All of your friends from high school are married and have children. You're going to have to come down from your high horse or you're going to be left all alone."

"I'd rather live alone than be miserable the rest of my life!" Rachel tried to control the raging feelings inside her.

"Well, if you keep this up, you might just get your wish!" She heard the phone click and then a dial tone.

Rachel hung up the phone in slow motion. She curled into the fetal position and let the tears come. Hot, angry tears coursed down her face, but no sobs. She picked up a pillow and threw it as hard as she could. It landed softly on the floor. Oblivious to how she looked, Rachel headed for the park. She stumbled blindly, reliving the conversation over again. It was a repeat of a hundred others, and every time it was like a knife stabbing her in the heart.

*God, why? Why does she do this? Is it too much to want a good, Christian man? One who loves me for who I am? Is there something wrong with me?* Questions and doubts clamored in her head, blocking out any communication.

Unwilling to go home or sit still, she plodded on until the descending darkness caused her to take a look at her surroundings. Nothing seemed familiar. She had wandered aimlessly, paying no attention to where she was headed, until nothing was recognizable. Rachel slowed to a stop in front of an old Victorian house. Something about it caught her eye. It was a house with character, a sense of history about it. That was one of the reasons she hated to see the Center destroyed—the way the past had made an impression on the very stone and wood. Even if her students were no longer interested in the building, she just couldn't stand to see such beauty go to waste.

She must have been standing there for several minutes because the porch light came on and the door squeaked open. Rachel's mouth dropped open when she recognized the owner.

"Evening, Rachel. What brings you to this part of town?" Rachel stared up at Randy in shock. He was the last person she would have expected to find here, and yet it seemed to fit perfectly. It was just the kind of house he would live in. She searched her mind for a reply.

She shrugged her shoulders and said, "I don't know. I went out for a walk, and I guess I just wandered around. I hadn't realized how far I'd come."

"Then, I guess you must be tired. Why don't you come in and rest for a minute?"

Rachel dug for an excuse, but couldn't find one. She was tired, but the shadows were still hiding her puffy eyes and rumpled appearance. If she went in, he was sure to ask questions that she wasn't ready to answer. He must have noticed her hesitation because he came down the steps to the gate.

"Come on in. I could use some advice."

"Advice?" Her confusion gave him enough time to

open the gate. Too late she realized the street lamp gave him a full view of her face.

"Hey! Are you all right?" he questioned, his eyes full of concern. He touched her arm and then pulled her gently into the gate. There was no use turning back now. Her worst fears had already come true. She might as well sit down and rest a minute. Somehow it was reassuring to have his arm supporting her, especially when her knees caved. "Whoa." He caught her with his other arm and lifted her easily into the air. She was so close that she could smell a mixture of cologne and fresh paint, an odd combination. He took her inside, depositing her on an antique couch.

"What's wrong? You look pale." Her stomach answered for her. She put a hand over it in embarrassment. "So that's it." His smile didn't hide the concern or the questions in his eyes, but he kept the latter to himself. "When's the last time you ate?"

"I guess breakfast."

"Well, then, I think you're overdue. I was just about to stop and eat myself. How about some takeout from that little Italian place? They deliver."

"I don't want to cause you any trouble."

He waved his hand as if to silence her. "It's no trouble. I need to eat too, and I would rather have company. Besides, I still need your expert advice."

"What about?"

"You'll see after dinner," he said. His face turned into a grim smile that caught at her heart. He walked back the way they had come. “Let me call in our order.” Then he was gone.

Rachel looked around at what was probably the living room or parlor. All the furniture was covered in the same burgundy velvet-like material. The wallpaper was a rose design in the same color with hints of blue and emerald. The rest of the room was oddly vacant. There were no drapes or rugs or pictures on the wall. It seemed so empty and hollow. Any further analysis was cut short by Randy’s return.

“Dinner will be here in about twenty minutes. Why don’t I get you something to drink and a snack until then?”

“Let’s just wait on dinner. Why don’t you give me a tour instead?”

“Sure.”

She followed him from room to room downstairs. All the rooms were done as far as painting and wallpapering, but they all shared the emptiness of the parlor. “Why aren’t there any pictures or rugs?” she finally asked.

“I’ve spent most of the last few months just getting the house in shape. I haven’t had time to decorate.” A shadow came over his face as he talked. “Besides, getting the remodeling done is more important now than decorating.”

“Why’s that?”

“You’re full of ‘why’s’ tonight, aren’t you?” She waited for him to answer. He ran his fingers through his hair. "If I take that position in Dothan, I'll need to have it looking good so I can sell it."

"Sell it?" Rachel protested. "How could you sell such a beautiful house? Especially since you put so much work into it."

"Well, it's too far to drive, and I can't afford to have two places. Selling is my only option."

"You could stay. Give me one good reason why you should leave." Before he had time to reply, the doorbell rang.

"Dinner's here." She watched him turn the corner.

"Saved by the bell," she whispered to herself.

❧

Randy watched her finish off the lasagna by wiping up the last of the sauce with a bite of garlic bread. She was really something. He was going to miss her smile and the way she enjoyed every bite. He wanted to drink in every detail of her face, from those blue eyes to those long legs. He didn't question her about why she'd been crying. Probably just a spat with what's-his-name. Rachel didn't need to worry—the guy was sure to come slithering back tomorrow. He wasn't going to waste precious time with Rachel thinking about that jerk. She pointed at his chest with her fork.

"Now, what was this expert advice you needed?"

"Follow me, and I'll show you." He started up the stairs, but realized halfway up that she wasn't with him. "Something wrong?" His brow furrowed in concern.

"You're not going to show me your etchings, are you?"

He laughed aloud and then put on his most serious face. "No. I want to show you my paint samples." He almost laughed at her dubious expression until he noticed she wasn't laughing. "Hey! I'm serious. I really want you to look at my paint samples. If it'll make you feel better, I'll bring them downstairs to the kitchen."

He watched her weigh the decision. With a guarded look she met him midway. "Show me your samples." It was almost a dare. He had never seen her act this way before.

"Right this way." He opened the master bedroom door with a flourish and waited for her to enter first. The guarded look turned to amusement. He pointed to a stack of paint samples on a rickety card table near the window. "I've been trying to pick the color of paint or wallpaper to use in here. That's why I was out walking this morning, trying to get a fresh perspective."

She bent over the samples and fingered a few. She stopped at a deep blue. "This is a beautiful color, but I wouldn't want it on the walls. It would be good for drapes, though." She flipped through the wallpaper samples and pointed to a small floral pastel print with a hint of the deeper blue in the design. "You could do the walls in this and the drapes and accessories in this." She pointed back to the blue that matched her eyes. He nodded in agreement.

"What about the bathroom?"

As she walked over, he noticed the amusement had turned into interest. She looked over the antique tub with the claw feet and the marble-looking sink with its brass fittings. He'd replaced the original ones with non-tarnishing fixtures. The floor was dark blue and white ceramic tile.

"I love this bathtub. And look, the color of the tiles is the same as the sample. It already blends with the bedroom samples."

He smiled at her excitement. He knew exactly how she felt. It was like bringing life to the house, one step at a time. "Now, see. You did in five minutes what I've been trying to do for two days. I just couldn't make up my mind."

"I'm glad to help." Her smile was warm, and the temptation to touch her hair was back. But she wasn't his. He'd just have to face it, but he couldn't do it with her looking at him like that. For a few precious moments he had dreamed that they were planning this as a team. This was exactly why he needed to move on. *If that were true,* a little voice said, *why haven't you put the house on the market?*

"Here, it's getting late. Let me give you a ride home."

# fifteen

On the ride home, Randy was very quiet. Rachel tried to think of something to say, but the silence was so heavy that she wasn't sure she could lift it even if she could think of something to talk about. They passed by the Center and she remembered their discussion from that morning.

"I called my students, like you suggested," she said.

"What did they say?" He glanced over at her and then back to the road.

"They all seemed to have found other activities or classes. It looks like I'm the only one who's missing the classes." She turned for a last look as the building faded into the night. "I don't know what to do now."

"Are you more upset about the building or losing your class?" he asked, giving her a sidelong glance.

"What do you mean?" she asked.

"What is more important to you, the building or helping people?" She looked at his profile, but couldn't discern the expression on his face. All she could see was the outline. She played with her seat belt.

"I don't know. It's a beautiful old building and I hate to see it go to waste. I also hate to see such good programs fall by the wayside." She was hedging the question.

"You still haven't answered my question," he said. The car pulled to a stop in front of her apartment. He turned in the seat and looked her full in the face, as if he were trying to see her soul. "What is bothering you the most?"

She looked down at her hands. She was afraid of giving something away. "Your leaving." It was out before she had a chance to think. Without another word she jumped out of the car and ran to her apartment door, not stopping until the door was firmly closed and locked behind her. She waited for his step on the walk, but there was nothing but silence. She held her breath for several minutes, releasing it in a sigh at the sound of his car pulling away.

How could she be so stupid? What made her say such a thing? *Because it's the truth,* a little voice replied. *It's the truth and you know it. You've really fallen for this guy.* The realization took her breath away. All this time she had put all her energy into Kyle, only to find out he was a jerk and a hypocrite. But Randy had been right there, waiting. He's such a gentleman, a gentle man. An even more shocking jolt was the realization that she had never even asked him about his relationship with Christ. She had assumed he was not a Christian because he was a professor, and most of the professors were not. Still, she hadn't once tried to witness to him. Then she remembered how he had said prayer was their only hope. Maybe he was a Christian. Still, it bothered her that she hadn't even asked.

Rachel picked up the pillow from the floor and curled up on the couch. How could she be so stupid? Randy had never once tried to take advantage of her like her so-called Christian friends. Susan was right. He was terrific. Now, what was she going to do? With a groan, she fell over onto the couch.

She must have been more tired than she felt because she awoke to the sun peeking through the windows. "It's Sunday!" she said out loud. She jumped up off the couch and checked the clock. She still had plenty of time to get ready for church. Church! Kyle! He was the last person she wanted to see, but there was no way around it. She had to face him. She wasn't going to spend the rest of her life running from him, or let him run her out of church.

A couple of hours later she stood, chin up and back straight at the church entrance. She jumped when a voice said, "You look like you're headed into battle, instead of church."

"Oh, Susan. It's only you." Rachel breathed a sigh of relief.

"Gee, thanks. I'm happy to see you too. Speaking of which, where have you been? I haven't seen you in ages."

"I'm sorry, Susan. It's been really weird, but I can't explain now. Let's go to lunch after church and I'll tell you all about it. Well, that is, if you have a couple of free days."

"I think I can clear my calendar," Susan replied.

Rachel could tell her curiosity was up now. "Let's go in. It's cold out here." Susan opened the door and propelled her inside, almost into Kyle's arms. Rachel was speechless.

"Hey, Kyle!" Susan said.

"Hi, Susan." Kyle refused to look up. "Rachel, can I talk to you for a minute?"

"I'll meet you guys inside," Susan said. She looked them both over as she made her way down the hall and into the classroom.

"Yes, Kyle." Rachel stood firm, both feet planted, ready for whatever he had to say.

"I'm sorry for the misunderstanding the other night. It won't happen again." He shifted his weight.

"You're right about that."

Kyle's head jerked up. "I said I was sorry. Look, can't we try this again? You know, from the beginning." He was almost begging. Rachel was suddenly cold all over. This wasn't the Kyle she had adored from afar. She didn't know who this guy was. Right now all she felt was pity.

"It's over, Kyle. I really don't think it ever began," Rachel said. She turned toward the classroom. "Class is about to start. I'll see you around."

She didn't dare look back. The last thing she needed right now was to feel sorry for him. She might fall back into that old routine of puppy love. On second thought, no, she couldn't fall for that again. She'd finally met someone who was real and whose character outshone the imaginary one she had made for Kyle. This was definitely over. Oddly, all she felt was relief. With a lighter heart, she joined Susan in class. Kyle disappeared.

Over lunch, Rachel told Susan all about the last few weeks, except the phone call from her mother. Susan's mouth dropped open as she slapped Rachel's arm in excitement.

"I can't believe you didn't call and tell me about this!" Susan exclaimed.

"Careful. You're going to leave bruises," Rachel replied, pushing the offending hand away. "It all happened so fast, and you were busy looking for another job. Speaking of which, have you found something?"

"Quit changing the subject. Yes I have, but I want to hear more about you and Randy."

"You've heard about all there is to tell. He's leaving." Rachel played with the food on her plate.

"He said he might leave if he took the job. It hasn't even been offered yet. Besides, I don't think he really wants to go, especially after what you told me about the house."

"Well then, why is he talking about leaving?" Rachel sputtered in exasperation.

"Beats me, but I think you ought to find out."

"Like I'm going to walk up and ask him."

"Why not?" Susan asked. "You'll never know until you do."

Rachel shook her head and took another sip of her tea. "Tell me about your job prospects." Susan gave her an

"I know what you're doing and it doesn't fool me" look and then plunged into the details about a possible job at a local school.

Rachel tried to show interest, but her mind was stuck on Randy. Why did he want to leave? It was obvious that he had ties here. What would make a man give up his house and job to go to another town? Rachel puzzled over it, but she couldn't come up with a good answer. A little hope started to burn in her heart. Maybe he was just lonely in that big old house. Maybe she could give him a reason to stay.

# sixteen

Monday morning Rachel's thoughts returned to Randy's question again and again, like a stuck record going around and around, but getting nowhere. What did she really want? Staring at another stack of essays to read, she sighed and plopped her head onto her arms. She really missed the interaction with her students from the community center. The way they tried so hard to learn to speak English. Most of her students at the university acted as if English were a foreign language, and from the look of their papers it might as well be one. What was with her lately, anyway? As the semester went by, she could dream of nothing but summer. Maybe she had spring fever. Maybe she just needed a break from Freshman Composition. With another sigh, she picked up her red pen and marked their papers until they looked like bloodstains.

"Excuse me. Are you Ms. Grant?"

Rachel looked up to see an elderly lady standing in the doorway. Though she must have been near seventy, she stood ramrod straight and wore an elegant suit. Rachel realized she was staring, so she stood up and crossed the room.

"Yes, I'm Rachel Grant. What can I do for you?"

"Are you the young woman who has been teaching at the community center?" The woman looked her up and down, as if trying to find a flaw.

"Yes, I am." Rachel waited for her to continue, but the woman just stared at her. Rachel cleared her throat.

"You look a little young to be teaching at a university," the woman replied.

"I assure you I have adequate credentials." Rachel refused to tell the woman her age. She was somewhere between being pleased that she looked young, and angry at the woman's snooty attitude. "Now, what can I do for you Ms. . ." Rachel trailed off, waiting for her to give her name.

"I'm Ms. Stanford." She emphasized the Ms. "Ms. Emily Stanford. I work with the local historical society. I heard that you were trying to get the community center designated a historical landmark. Is that true?"

"Yes, ma'am, I am." Rachel's heart began to race. Maybe there was still a way to save the Center, but she could tell there would be no rushing Ms. Stanford. "Is the society rethinking the proposal?"

"No. The society's decision is final. There is no funding available at present." Rachel's heart plummeted. "However," Mrs. Stanford said and then paused, one finger pointing at Rachel. "However, I might be interested in the project myself." Before Rachel could say a word she rushed on, "Now, mind you, I'm not one for rushing into things. I want to know exactly why you want to renovate the Center and what you are going to do with it."

"I really didn't have any plans, Ms. Stanford." Rachel found herself stumbling over words and trying to think of something that would satisfy this woman. "I was only a teacher there. I just think it's a great building architecturally, and it was a place for the community, a place for the kids to play and to learn." Rachel shrugged her shoulders for lack of words. "I don't know what else to tell you."

"You've told me enough for now, but I want a complete proposal of what you intend to do with the Center in my hands no later than tomorrow night. I expect you and Dr. Harris to give me a full report at dinner. Here's my card. We eat at six-thirty sharp. Don't be late." With a nod, she exited the room at a marching step.

Rachel stood in stunned silence. Tomorrow night! How in the world was she going to have a proposal ready for tomorrow night! She knew less than nothing about proposals, much less what she would plan for the Center. All she wanted was her old job back. What was she going to do? Panic rose from deep within. Then she remembered what Ms. Stanford had said. She had included Randy in this meeting. She threw the papers into her bag and ran for his office.

❧

Randy almost dropped the book he was previewing when Rachel skidded to a halt in front of his desk. "Randy, I need your help." Her breath was coming in short gasps.

"Slow down. Breathe in and out. Now, sit down and tell me what's wrong." Randy came around the desk and pulled her onto the small couch.

"Ms. Stanford needs a proposal by tomorrow night, and I can't do it by myself," she burst out.

"Whoa! Who's Ms. Stanford and what proposal?" Randy shook his head in confusion. "What are you talking about?"

"A few minutes ago, a woman named Emily Stanford came to my classroom and said she was interested in helping with the Center if we would give her a proposal of how we want to renovate and what we plan to do with the Center. Only she wants it by dinner tomorrow night. We're supposed to be there, ready to report at six-thirty sharp." Rachel barely breathed between words.

"Us? Why does she want us to give her a proposal?" Randy asked.

"I don't know. She just came and announced it a few minutes ago. She didn't give me an opportunity to ask any questions. Besides, I was too stunned to ask. She said she was a member of the historical society."

"That's right! Ms. Stanford." Randy replied, shaking his head. "She was one of the people I talked to about the Center. At the time, she didn't seem particularly interested."

"Well, something has gotten her interest, and we don't have any time to lose. Will you help me?" Rachel asked. He looked into her pleading eyes and knew there was only one answer.

"Of course I will. We'll get on it right after my last class. We can work on it at my place."

"Great. I'll meet you here after class." Her smile lit up the room. She squeezed his arm. "Thank you." Then she jumped up and sprinted back down the hall.

He knew he should stay away from her, but he couldn't say no to her. She needed him right now, and that was reason enough. In a few weeks, the university would be making its final decisions regarding the satellite school. After that, all he would have of Rachel would be memories.

Time seemed to move slowly for Randy the rest of the day. Finally, class was over and he could get back to Rachel. He found her pacing in front of his office like a caged cat.

"I guess I don't have to ask if you're ready to go." He expected a smile or a laugh, but not a look of pure panic. "Hey, it's going to be all right." Randy took her by the shoulders and looked into her eyes. "We can do this. But if we don't, we're just back to where we were yesterday."

When she only shrugged, he opened his office and drew her inside and closed the door. With one smooth move he pulled her into his arms, nestling her head against his shoulder. He stroked her hair gently with one hand, and held her firmly with the other. It felt so right to hold her. She snuggled against him and buried her head deeper into his shoulder. He held on for a few moments, wanting to ease her fears. How could something feel so right and be wrong?

She pulled back and looked up at him with those eyes. He felt like he was being sucked under. Before he could think about it, he leaned down and pressed his lips to hers. When she responded, he kissed her thoroughly. He wasn't sure how long they stood embracing, but a sudden knock sent them to separate corners. Gathering his senses about him, he took care of the student waiting outside, and then motioned for Rachel to follow.

"Let's go. We have a lot of work to do."

❧

In her own car, Rachel followed Randy's sedan into the driveway. All the way over she had replayed the scene in his office. She shivered with pleasure. He hadn't been all hands and groping. It had been romantic and sweet. She was surprised at the way she had responded. She had never felt that way before. His touch had left her breathless and weak-kneed. She hugged herself as she waited for Randy to open the door. He held the door for her, but he seemed to be standing as far away from her as possible. Her brows furrowed in confusion as she walked past into the foyer.

"Why don't we work at the kitchen table? It's probably the only flat, clean surface in the house." She thought perhaps he was joking, but the smile didn't quite reach his eyes. He pulled out a chair for her and then moved to the opposite side of the table.

"How should we start this?" Rachel asked. She threw her hands up in the air and scrunched her shoulders in puzzlement.

"Why don't we start with dinner? I'll call in our order. The usual?" he asked.

She nodded her head in agreement. Watching the way he jumped up and went into the other room, it seemed as if he couldn't wait to get away from her. What was wrong with him? She heard the phone ring before he called the restaurant. It was obviously a student with a problem. Not many teachers took the time to talk with students at home. Figuring he would be busy for several minutes and too fidgety to sit still, she decided to see how the bedroom was coming. He found her there a few minutes later.

"What do you think?" he asked.

She looked around at the half-finished room. Rolls of the wallpaper she had picked out were stacked neatly in the corner. He had finished two of the four walls.

"I like it. It's going to look really good when you add the drapes and furniture." She waved her hand at the room, void of any furniture, except the rickety card table and two sawhorses. He laughed, but didn't reply. She couldn't take this anymore.

"Randy, what's wrong?"

"What do you mean?"

"I mean ever since our kiss this afternoon you've been acting funny, like you don't want to be around me. I don't understand." He colored at the mention of their touch.

"This afternoon was a mistake. I shouldn't have done that and I apologize."

An apology was the last thing she wanted, but she held her tongue. She swallowed the lump that was forming in her throat. "Oh." That was all she could get out. It sounded so lame. She tried again. "I guess you're right. We are colleagues."

"Right," he said too quickly. "We should keep our relationship professional, but friendly. Speaking of work, we'd better get to it."

She followed him downstairs to the kitchen, and they began discussing the details of the renovations that needed to be made to the Center. Randy made a list of materials they would need as they went.

"I guess that the biggest thing is the roof, especially where the tree went through my classroom. I noticed that they had removed the tree and pulled up the stump. The inside and outside stairs need to be repaired. A good coat of paint would be nice, and the floors need stripping."

"Hold on. You're going too fast." He scribbled a few things down on paper with his right hand while he held his left hand up like a stop sign. He lowered it and said, "Okay. Go ahead."

She went on with her wish list of the things she wanted to see done to the Center, and Randy continued to scribble for a few minutes, and then pulled out a clean sheet of paper. He organized the repairs to be made in order of importance, and on another sheet he listed the materials necessary.

"That should do it. We can type it up at school tomorrow. That was the easy part. Now you've got to decide what you want to use the Center for."

"What do you mean me? What about us?" She looked up in surprise.

"I mean that the Center is yours, not mine. I won't be here. Remember?" She was relieved from having to answer by the ringing of the doorbell. "Saved by the bell. Again." He went to the door to get the food.

She remained at the kitchen table, a wave of nausea flowing through her. He was really going to leave. The kiss this afternoon meant nothing to him. He was still leaving her. It stunned her how much it hurt to think of him leaving. Just when she realized what a wonderful man he was, he was moving out of her life. She struggled to gain her composure when she heard his steps in the hall.

"Here we are. Lasagna for two."

He placed the food out on the table and they ate in silence. Randy tried once or twice to talk of school or the weather, but she couldn't get words past that lump in her throat. She put her fork down a few minutes later, and pushed the half-eaten plate away.

"I've had enough."

"You've barely touched it. Are you all right?" The concern in his eyes was almost her undoing, but she swallowed down the tears.

"I'm just not hungry tonight. I had a big lunch." It was a lie, but it was better than telling the truth. She wasn't hungry because the only man she had ever loved was about to walk out of her life. "Let's get back to work."

Randy took the plates to the kitchen sink and wiped

off the table. Sitting down at the table, he pushed the notepad across the table to her.

"This part is all yours."

She looked at the blank page and thought of the Center and her students. If Randy was going to leave, the only thing she had left was the Center. It was a place she could do something that meant more than just earn a paycheck. She thought of all her students and all the kids that played there in the afternoons.

"Well, first, I would want to restart the conversational English classes, and the after school program for children." She wrote that down on the paper.

"What else?" he prodded. "Isn't there something you would like to see them do that they're not doing now?"

"Yeah. GED and adult education classes." She added it to the list. One idea sparked another until there was a page full of ideas. When she put her pen down, he added the renovation lists to her sheet and handed them to her.

"You type better than I do." He smiled and patted her hand. "You did a good job, now you can relax." He looked at the clock and frowned. "It's late. Maybe I should follow you home."

"No. I'm fine," Rachel protested. "It's not that late." Gathering up the papers, she moved toward the front door. "I'll do these first thing in the morning and leave a copy in your office for you to proof."

"Sure. That'll be great."

"Bye." She fled. He called a soft good-bye from the

porch, but she was intent on escape. She backed the car out of the driveway and headed for home without looking back. The tears were already beginning to fall, and she didn't want him to see her cry. Pity was the last thing she needed.

# seventeen

Rachel rushed to the university computer lab and found the first PC in sight. She only had ten minutes to type up the proposal before class. She had cut the alarm off in her sleep the night before and had awakened to sun streaming through the window, which was not good. Looking down at her jeans and oversized sweater, she frowned. Everything in her closet had been wrinkled or was dirty. Her hair had not cooperated, so it was pulled back into a bow at the base of her neck. She typed with a fury, groaning at every mistake. She finished and sent it to the printer, but there were two students ahead of her who were finishing up their term papers, just in time for class. She tapped her foot until her ankle started to ache. Finally, the printer spit it out. She glanced over it, saved the file to a disk, and headed for Randy's office. She was going to be a few minutes late, but the students would get over it. Half of them never showed up on time anyway. Randy's office was locked so she slid the proposal under his door with a sigh and went to class.

She fumbled through her classes, anxious to get back with Randy. It wasn't because of the proposal, she admitted to herself, but because she wanted to see him again. She wanted to see if he really meant what he said last night about leaving, or if he was only trying to protect himself. More than anything, she wanted to see that look in his eyes again. The one that said he wanted her. She stopped by his office between every class, but missed him every time. Deep inside, she knew he was hiding from her. She finally saw him at the lunch break.

"Randy," she called. Rachel jogged down the hall to where he stood with one hand on the door. "I've been trying to catch you all morning." She paused for a breath. "Did you read over the proposal?"

"It looks fine." He didn't say anything more, and Rachel knew he was sticking to his plan. He wouldn't even look her in the eye. "Look, I've got to go now. I'm meeting someone for lunch."

"Oh, sure. I understand." She felt a pain in her chest, a tightness, like someone was trying to squeeze the life out of her. "You are still going with me to meet Ms. Stanford tonight, aren't you?" He looked up then.

"Of course. I told you I would." He seemed almost hurt by the accusation in her voice. "I'll come by your house about six, and we can ride over together."

"Great. I'll see you at six, then." He nodded and disappeared through the door. She wondered who he was meeting for lunch. Maybe that person was the reason he didn't want to continue what happened last night. Maybe that was why he wanted to move. Possibilities flew around in her head until she was dizzy. It could be anything, and these mind games were getting her nowhere. She repositioned her bag and followed him out the door. She had to eat something, or she would never make it through her last class. She made her way across the quad to The Magnolia.

Rachel didn't see them until she had picked up her order and was looking for a table. Randy was sitting at their table with a knockout. She was tall and willowy, making Rachel feel suddenly awkward and ugly in her jeans and sweater. The woman was wearing a tailored suit and French heels in the latest style. Randy was leaning across the table, following her every word. She had been right—he was seeing someone else. Kissing Rachel had just been a passing whim, an emotional moment. Why would he want Rachel, when he could have this blond beauty?

Her stomach tightened, and all desire for food left. She made her way to a table half-hidden by a fake tree and forced herself to eat. She had barely forced down two bites when Jane Coefield, secretary to the Dean of the English Department, slid into the chair opposite her.

"Hey, Rachel. Is this chair free?" She settled in without waiting for Rachel to answer. Looking around, Rachel noticed that most of the tables were full, so she could hardly ask to be left alone.

"Sure, Jane."

"Did you see that woman with Dr. Harris? She's something else, isn't she?" Jane scowled at the woman's back. "She's been with Dr. Harris all afternoon, hanging on him like a long-lost love. Her name's Kathryn Dawson and from what I overheard, she's from Dothan where they're talking about building the satellite school."

Jane prattled on, but Rachel didn't hear anymore. Her worst dreams were coming true. Kathryn was the reason he was so intent on moving. The food in Rachel's stomach turned to stone, but she forced the remaining few bites down her throat. She made all the right replies to Jane's remarks and left as fast as she could.

❧

Randy listened to Kathryn rave on and on about her plans for him once he moved to Dothan to work at the new satellite school. She always had been a take-charge person. Even when they were little, she had tried to run the house and tell him what to do. Although he was older by two years, she thought she had to take care of him.

"Randy, dear, are you listening to me?" She tapped her nails on the table in front of him.

"Of course I am, sister dear. I was just thinking about when you were a little girl. Now look at you, all grown up and running your own business." She smiled up at him.

"That's more like it." Kathryn leaned back in her chair and eyed him critically. "What's wrong?" Randy twisted in his seat, but refused to meet her gaze.

"What do you mean? Everything's great. After this semester, I'll probably be starting a great new job and be living down the road from you and Michael. What else could I ask for?"

"I can tell something is wrong. You can't hide anything from me, brother dear, so spill it," Kathryn drawled, tapping the table for emphasis.

"Like I said before, everything's fine."

"Don't give me that, Randy. I've seen this look before, but I've never seen it this bad." Kathryn took a sip of her iced tea and watched him over the rim. She waited for him to answer.

"I'm just worried about a friend, that's all."

"Is this a girl-kind-of-friend?" Kathryn asked slyly.

"Never mind," Randy replied.

"I can't help you if you don't tell me what's wrong," Kathryn complained.

They spent the rest of the meal in quiet. Kathryn was pouting. Sometimes she didn't know when to let things drop. He tried to make small talk about the view and the food, but his mind wandered back to last night. Rachel had been responsive to his touch. There was still a chance that she didn't really love that guy. God would just have to work things out, and if she decided to stay with the jerk, then so be it. Then he would take the job and start fresh somewhere else. With the decision made, he felt a load fall from his shoulders. He stood up and gave Kathryn a hug.

"You're something else."

"I know." She gave him a crooked smile. She kissed him gently on the cheek. "Maybe someday you'll tell me what's bothering you." They parted company at the door, leaving Randy alone with his thoughts. He would just have to give it to God and let Him handle it.

# eighteen

Rachel spent the rest of the afternoon in a mental fog of doubt, worry, and pure jealousy. No matter how she tried, she couldn't get the image of Randy and that woman out of his mind. How could she compete with that blond goddess? She pulled into her apartment's parking lot, but couldn't remember any of the drive home. By five-thirty she was a knot of nerves. Randy arrived precisely at six o'clock, not too early and not too late. With one hand on the doorknob, she tried for a deep breath, but only managed a shaky gasp. "Pull yourself together, girl," she muttered aloud. The doorbell rang again, and she jumped, jerking the door open. Randy stared in startled surprise.

"Are you all right?" he asked. He looked handsome in a collarless dress shirt and sports jacket. The navy blue brought out his brown eyes.

"Fine. The bell just startled me." She tried to laugh it off, but she could feel him watching her.

"Are you ready?"

"As ready as I'll ever be. Did the proposal look okay?" Rachel asked. He opened the briefcase at his side. The case looked new and expensive. Rachel couldn't remember seeing it before. "Is that a new briefcase?"

"Yes, it is. Kathryn gave it to me."

"Oh." She couldn't think of anything to say. The mere mention of Kathryn's name had sent a flush of heat to her cheeks. "It's very nice."

"Yes, it is," he mumbled as he searched through the papers. Finally, he pulled out three bound copies of the report. She hadn't even thought of that. He gave one copy to Rachel. "Here's your copy. You can look it over on the way to Ms. Stanford's house."

"First, there's something I've been meaning to ask you." Rachel took a deep breath and gathered her courage. "I realized the other day that I had failed in my duty as a friend and as a Christian." She paused for a moment.

"Go on," Randy said, looking intently at her.

"Are you a Christian?" She glanced out from under her lashes and was surprised by the warm smile on his face. It had been several days since she had seen that smile.

"Yes, I am." He shook his head. "I'm guilty of the same. You mentioned God answering your prayers, so I assumed you were a Christian. I never asked, either, but I'm glad you did."

"Well, now that that's out of the way let's go charm Ms. Stanford." She sounded more convincing than she felt.

She followed Randy out, taking an extra moment as she locked the door to calm her racing heart. He was a Christian. That was one more reason to love him. As she walked around him to the car, their shoulders brushed, and a shiver ran up her spine. He pretended not to notice, but he stepped away a little too quickly so she was certain he'd felt it too. Rachel could feel her stomach knot up and her face burn. Now that he had Kathryn, he couldn't even stand to touch her. She watched him settle into the driver's seat, and she didn't take her eyes off of him until they pulled into Ms. Stanford's driveway. Tonight might be her last night with him, she realized. She felt compelled to take in every inch of his profile, every mannerism.

"We're here." Randy's voice broke her concentration. She picked up the report and what was left of her composure and got out of the car. Randy followed her up the stairs. They seemed so steep, yet they arrived at the door too soon. When the butler answered the bell, Rachel almost turned tail and ran. Almost.

"Please follow me," the butler requested. She was tempted to mock his tight-jointed walk like they did in the cartoons. Instead, Rachel walked calmly in his wake. His broad back blocked her view of the room until he stepped aside. She almost gasped at the sight. It was a library, but the word hardly described the place. It was more a haven for books, books, and more books. Floor-to-ceiling bookshelves lined the circular room, except in the center of the far wall where it stopped at a massive fireplace and on each side where bay windows stood as sentinels. On one side a black lacquered grand piano was placed at an angle. In the middle a Queen

Anne sofa and wingback chairs surrounded the fireplace. On the right, a massive cherry desk faced the room. Emily Stanford was seated in the leather chair behind it, looking more formidable than ever. Rachel took a deep breath and went to the seat the butler indicated. The clock chimed the half hour as Ms. Stanford looked up from the papers she had been reading.

"Did you bring the report?" Ms. Stanford asked.

"Yes. It's right here." Rachel fumbled in her briefcase until she remembered that Randy had Ms. Stanford's copy in his case. "Uhm. Dr. Harris has it." She tried to cover her embarrassment, but she could feel the heat in her cheeks.

"Here you go, Mrs. Stanford," Randy said as he handed her the report.

"That's *Ms.* Stanford." She emphasized the Ms. with all the starch of a military dress uniform.

"Sorry," Randy mumbled.

"I'll look this over and then we can discuss it at length over dinner. Miles will show you to the dining room."

The butler appeared at Rachel's right. Ms. Stanford turned to the manuscript without another word. Rachel followed Miles into the dining room. "Ms. Stanford will join you shortly," Miles said and then disappeared as quickly as he appeared. She stood in the doorway uncertain of what to do.

"She's not long on ceremony, is she? Or small talk, for that matter," Randy whispered. When she didn't answer, Randy continued, "Look. Everything will be okay. Don't let her get to you."

"Easy for you to say."

"Hey, we're in this together. Remember?"

"Yeah, but for how long?"

Randy didn't have time to respond before Ms. Stanford swept into the room and motioned for them to take seats at the table. As soon as they were seated, she rang the bell at her side and a maid materialized with the first course.

"I was impressed with your report, Ms. Grant, and you too, Dr. Harris." She paused to take a bite of salad. Rachel followed suit with a prayer that she didn't drip dressing all over herself. "I've decided to buy the Center."

Rachel almost choked on the broccoli she was carefully chewing. "Excuse me?" she managed to squeak.

"I've decided to buy the Center property. I called the city and asked them to put a hold on the demolition until I could meet with them to discuss terms." Rachel stared at the woman in disbelief. Her cold blue eyes were as sharp as steel and unwavering. "I will have my executor handle the money for the renovation. I will forward your ideas to him, and he will have the final say regarding the project. However, there is one thing. I expect Ms. Grant to meet with me once a week to keep me informed. Is that clear?"

For the first time, Ms. Stanford looked up from her food and stared directly into her eyes. Rachel swallowed hard. "Why me?"

"Because you will be the director."

Rachel wasn't sure if she had heard correctly. Director? What did she mean, director? "Ms. Stanford, I'm no director. I'm a teacher. Susan is the director."

"I contacted Susan, but she has already accepted a position at the high school. Besides, you are my first choice."

"But, Ms. Stanford, I don't have any experience in administration," Rachel protested.

"Let's get one thing straight, Ms. Grant. Either you are the director, or I withdraw funding. Are we understood?"

Rachel stared, mouth open, for several moments. Ms. Stanford's eyes locked with hers, and she knew she had no choice. "Yes, ma'am."

"Good. I'll expect you Monday after your class to discuss the details."

That was all Ms. Stanford said during dinner. Randy didn't say a word until they were on their way down the sidewalk.

"Well, it looks like you get to keep the Center."

Rachel couldn't think of an answer. They drove to her apartment in silence. She barely heard Randy's goodbye. She unlocked the apartment and dressed for bed in a daze. It was only eight o'clock, but she couldn't handle anything else tonight. She needed time to take it all in and digest it. What exactly did Ms. Stanford mean by director? Rachel was sure to find out on Monday.

# nineteen

Wednesday dawned bright and clear, but Rachel's head was as a fuzzy as a teddy bear. It wasn't until she looked at the calendar that the significance of the date hit her. Today was her birthday. Her thirtieth birthday. Rachel suddenly felt the need to sit down. She didn't feel thirty. How was it possible? Her reverie was broken by the shrill ring of the telephone.

"Hello."

"Hi, sweetheart. How's the birthday girl?" Rachel moaned inwardly. Her mother's cheery voice was the last thing she needed to hear this morning.

"I'm fine, Mom."

"Well, you don't sound fine."

"I just got up. I'm still a little groggy."

"Well, get up and at 'em. Today's your day. I just wanted to make sure what time you eat lunch."

"Why?" Rachel questioned.

"Because it's your birthday and I'm going to take you to lunch."

"Mom, you don't have to do that. A phone call is all that's necessary." Rachel prayed that her mother would take the hint. No such luck.

"Don't be silly. I can't let you celebrate your birthday alone. I'll meet you at the school at noon in the lobby."

"Mom, you really don't have to come all the way up here. Really. I'm fine."

"Now, that's enough. It's already decided. I'll see you at twelve. Bye."

The phone clicked before Rachel could open her mouth again. She sank back into the chair and gave her moan full vocal range. A birthday dinner. Just what she needed. Dragging herself back to the bathroom, she took her time getting dressed for work.

The day went from bad to worse. By the time her first class was over, she was ready to go home and back to bed. It started with an innocent remark made by an unsuspecting student. It was about twenty minutes before the end of class, and Rachel had decided to let them out early so that she could get this birthday lunch over with as soon as possible.

"Since it's my birthday, I'm letting class go early today," Rachel said. Cheers and applause broke out across the room.

"How old are you?" Steven asked. "Thirty-four or thirty-five?"

Rachel had turned to clean the blackboard, but stopped in midswipe and stared at the board. Without looking around she ground out, "I'm thirty, thank you very much."

Several of the students booed Steven. One even cuffed

the side of his head as they headed out of the classroom. Steven stopped at her desk on his way out.

"Sorry about that, Ms. Grant. You look good for your age." She whirled around as he tried to dig his way out of the situation. "I mean. . .I mean you. . .I'm sorry." He looked pitiful, but Rachel was in no mood to be kind. She just stared him down. He backed his way out of the room saying, "I'm sorry" so many times that she thought she would scream.

After that, she went into the faculty restroom and took a good long look in the mirror. She didn't see any wrinkles or crow's feet, but her eyes were puffy and her make-up looked smeared. She tried to fix it, but ended up making it look caked on instead. Rachel was about to leave when something shiny caught her eye. At first she thought it was a piece of tinsel, but a second glance showed a silvery hair mixed in with the brown. She yanked it out and stared at it. Not another one. She stared in disbelief at the mirror. A closer inspection showed several more scattered throughout. She was too young to have gray hair. Make that silver hair. This stuff glowed in the dark.

A glance at her watch sent her scurrying toward the lobby. The last thing she needed was a lecture on being late. She had spent way too much time staring into the mirror. Rachel entered the lobby just as the bell tower struck the noon hour. She spotted her mother sitting on a couch in the corner, her foot tapping time. Taking a deep breath, Rachel steeled herself and crossed the room, all the while repeating, "Stay calm" to herself.

"Hi, Mom." She plastered a smile to her face and accepted a hug.

"Hi, dear. How's the birthday girl?" Her mom's voice was a little too perky.

"You already asked me that, but I'm fine. Where do you want to go for lunch?" Rachel asked.

"That's up to you. It's your birthday."

"Fine. Let's go to The Magnolia."

"The Magnolia? Isn't that the little restaurant here on campus?"

"Yes it is. Is that a problem?" Rachel ground out.

"Well, no. If that's where you really want to go, then let's go. I just thought you might want to go to a nice restaurant downtown."

"I like The Magnolia and it's close. Traffic is bad this time of day."

"Fine. Fine," her mom replied. Rachel could tell she was disappointed, but it was her choice and she had made it. For once her mother would just have to accept it. "Let's go, then." She said it with a smile, but Rachel could tell that her mom was playing the sacrificial lamb to the hilt.

The walk across the quad was filled with idle chatter, mostly from her mom. Edna Grant could be quite a gossip. She knew more about the school and the community events than the people involved in them, and she was determined to tell Rachel all of it before they reached the restaurant. They ordered and then took the trays to a table near the corner. Edna was still spouting gossip like a perpetual water fountain even as they sat down. Rachel was so lost in her own thoughts that she was startled to hear Randy's voice.

"I thought I saw you come in." She could feel the warmth of his hand on her shoulder. She turned to answer him, but nothing came out. His face was only inches from hers. Her mother answered for her.

"I don't believe we've met. I'm Edna Grant, Rachel's mother." She held out her hand and Randy took it with a smile.

"It's nice to meet you, Mrs. Grant."

"Call me Edna."

"Edna." He nodded. "I'll let you two ladies get back to your lunch."

"Oh, please stay," Edna begged. "It's Rachel's birthday, and it would be so nice to have some of her friends here. More like a party. I rarely get to meet her friends from here." To Rachel's ears it sounded more like an accusation than an invitation, but then again, she was used to it.

"Why don't you stay, Randy?" Rachel gave him smile and patted the seat between them. She wasn't sure whether it was a good idea or not. His presence might tame her mother's tongue, but on the other hand, it might just be more embarrassing. Either way, she didn't want to be rude to Randy.

"Well, if you put it that way, I'll go get my tray." He looked as uncertain as Rachel felt. He returned in a moment with his food and sat down between them.

"Randy is it?" her mother asked. It was just her way of forcing out more details.

"Dr. Randall Harris, this is my mother, Edna Grant. Mom, this is Dr. Harris."

"Randy is fine," he replied.

"So what do you do, Randy?" her mother inquired.

"I'm an English professor."

"Well, how did you meet Rachel?"

"Mom," Rachel complained, "we're not playing twenty questions. Let him eat his lunch." Rachel smiled an apology at Randy.

"I just wanted to get to know your friends a little better," her mother admonished.

The rest of lunch was spent in idle chitchat with Randy bearing the brunt of the conversation. Edna was sulking, and Rachel couldn't seem to think of anything to say. Randy finished lunch in record time and then made his excuses.

"It was nice meeting you, Mrs. Grant. Happy birthday, Rachel." He brushed her shoulders with his fingertips and then disappeared. She wished she could disappear like a magician's assistant.

"Well, I hope you're satisfied with yourself, young lady," her mother huffed.

"What do you mean?" Rachel asked the question, but she already knew the answer.

"A nice, eligible man and you sit there like a knot on a log. How do you ever expect to catch a husband by cowering in a corner?"

"Mother, finding someone to spend the rest of your life with is not like picking out melons at the grocery store. It takes time. Besides, I'm not trying to catch Randy," she lied. The last thing she was going to do was to give her mother the satisfaction of knowing she had been dumped again. "He's got a gorgeous girlfriend and he's moving away after this semester."

There she had said it, but it still hurt to hear the words out loud. She had to face facts. He was involved with someone else, and he was planning to move to be closer to her. Rachel's mother was still fuming silently. Rachel could imagine wisps of smoke coming out her ears and nostrils, just like a steam engine. The image brought an unexpected smile to her face which only made Edna angrier.

"What are you smiling at? Do you like making me miserable? Hmmm? Well, the joke's on you. You're the one who's going to spend the rest of her life alone." Edna grabbed her purse with a flourish and left a wounded Rachel alone at the table.

She knew she should go after her mother, but she didn't have the strength left to fight. She was an old maid and she might as well get used to the idea. She tried to think of the positive side of being independent, like freedom to do whatever she wanted. Yet, hard as she tried, nothing could take away the knot in her stomach or the lethargy that seemed to be taking over her body. All she wanted to do was go home and go to bed.

That wasn't to be. On her way out, she almost ran into Randy and Kathryn in the parking lot. She was curled onto his arm like a parasitic vine. Rachel mentally slapped herself for the thought. It wasn't the woman's fault that she was beautiful and could have any man she wanted, while an old maid like herself only attracted jerks and morons. She waited behind the shrubs until they got into his car and pulled away.

Rachel tried to shake her gloomy mood on the ride home, but those ugly phrases kept coming back to her. *Are you thirty-four or thirty-five? You're going to end up all alone.* By the time she pulled into her parking space, the tears were just below the surface. She made it into her apartment before she embarrassed herself completely. Ten minutes of uncontrolled tears and sobbing only gave her a headache instead of the release of her frustrations.

She flipped over on her side to reach for the tissues on her nightstand, but found instead her Bible which was buried under a stack of books. It had been a while since she had really read her Bible, or prayed, for that matter. She held the leather volume in her hands and prayed for help. She didn't know what else to pray. Then she flipped the Bible open at random and started reading the thirty-seventh chapter of Isaiah. It was about how King Hezekiah was being threatened by the Assyrians who had conquered many peoples. The Assyrian spokesman, Rabshakeh, said that God could not protect them. Hezekiah was depressed and frightened, but he went to the Lord with his fears. Rachel realized that her situation was very similar. She was being attacked by words and her own fears. She needed to trust in God, that He would never leave her alone. He would always be there. She looked back down, and the words of verse six leaped off the page. "Be not afraid of the words that thou hast heard. . ." In that instant, Rachel knew the Lord was speaking to her. Don't believe the words of others. Believe the word of God. He had always been faithful before, and He would be faithful again.

She marked the verse with a slip of paper, then closed the Bible. She hugged it to herself and prayed for guidance. God had something planned for her life, but maybe it wasn't the plans that she had made for herself.

"What should I do?" Rachel prayed.

*"If any man has ought against you, go and make it right."*

*Mother.* Rachel rebelled at the thought. Mother should come to her. She was the one who started it all. She was always putting Rachel down and making her feel unlovable. But that still, small voice wouldn't leave her head. Rachel knew that she would have to confront her mother.

They had to settle this once and for all or she would never know true peace. Rachel bowed her head and asked for strength and guidance. Tomorrow after class, she would go home and try to make her understand.

Rachel went to bed that night with the knowledge that things were out of her hands. God was in control and He would do what was best for everybody. For the first night in forever, she fell into a deep, restful sleep.

# twenty

On the long drive down, Rachel tried to think of what to say to her mother, what approach to take. Anything she said was bound to make her angry or hurt. She kept tossing scenarios around in her mind, but all of them ended in a fight. She prayed with her eyes open, knowing that God would have to give her the words today or she would surely louse things up.

Her mother's car was in the driveway, so at least she was home. Rachel wasn't sure if she was happy or disappointed. Her stomach felt like a huge knot, and her mouth was so dry that she couldn't swallow. She took a deep breath and went inside, knocking gently as she opened the door.

"Mama, are you here? It's me. Rachel." She heard a muffled voice from the kitchen and followed the sound. "Mama?"

When she pushed the door open, her mother jumped back with a cry, her hand over her heart. Then she reached for a chair and released a sigh.

"Rachel, don't ever sneak up on your mother that way. You nearly gave me a heart attack. You of all people should know better than to walk in unannounced in a lady's house, especially one who lives alone." She pulled out a chair and sat down, taking a moment to catch her breath. "If I had a gun, I could have killed you."

"Mama, you don't own a gun, and you don't know how to shoot one anyway," Rachel replied, taking the seat opposite her mother. Just like enemies at the bargaining table.

"Well, it's the principle of the thing." She straightened an imaginary wrinkle out of the tablecloth. Rachel could tell she was still angry about yesterday and was waiting for an apology.

"I didn't mean to scare you, Mother. I knocked, but you didn't answer. If you're so worried about someone breaking in, maybe you should lock the door." She could see her mother's back tensing, just like a cat about to attack. She had better back up and start over or they would be fighting again. "I just wanted to talk to you about yesterday."

"What about it? Did you come to yell some more?"

"I wanted to apologize for yelling, but I also want to clear the air about why I was so upset."

Her mother's shoulders relaxed a fraction, but she still wouldn't look Rachel in the eye. At least she was listening.

"Mama, what you said yesterday hurt me." That got her attention. Her mother turned with her mouth open wide. "Wait. Let me finish." Rachel looked down at the table and rolled the end of the tablecloth. "You make it sound like nobody would want me."

"I said no such thing."

"No, but you imply it by the way you are constantly thrusting guys at me, like I can't find my own boyfriend."

"That's because you never do."

"Mother, I don't want to rush into anything. I want to take my time and make sure I find the right guy. I'd rather be single than to be married and miserable," Rachel replied.

"That's fine, but you never go out. You sit at home alone or spend all your time at work. How are you ever going to meet someone just sitting at home?" her mother asked, exasperation evident in every word.

"When the time is right, God will put the right man in my path."

"Well, can't God use me to do that?"

"I guess so, but He hasn't," Rachel replied. "Besides, it's the way you do it, Mother. Tricking me into dates with guys I don't want to have anything to do with."

"What are you talking about? Dale is a nice young man and you barely gave him a chance. It takes time to get to know someone."

"Dale wasn't interested in getting to know me, Mother," Rachel ground out. "He had his mind on one thing, and it didn't require conversation."

The light came on in her mother's eyes. "Do you mean he tried to. . .that he. . ." Her mouth clamped shut. "That. . .that. . .oh, how dare he?" Rachel was surprised at the anger in her mother's voice. "He didn't hurt you, did he?"

"No." Rachel was a little confused. "No. I told him off the first time."

"That's why you wouldn't go with him for dessert." She looked at Rachel, understanding dawning in her eyes. "Why didn't you tell me this earlier?"

"I don't know. I guess I was embarrassed."

"Embarrassed? You didn't do anything wrong," she fumed. "Just wait till I get my hands on that boy."

"No, Mother. Just let it go. I just want to forget about him," Rachel cried. She smoothed the wrinkles in the tablecloth. "Besides, he's just like so many of the other guys."

"Not all men are like that, Rachel." Her mother reached across the table and patted her hand. Rachel looked up into her mother's eyes and for once there was no condemnation, no frustration. Only love. "The reason why I push you so much is that I don't want you to be alone. I know what it's like. I also know what it's like to share your life with someone you love. Your father was a wonderful man, and I miss him." She wiped the tears from her eyes.

"But, Mom, don't you see? That's the kind of relationship I want. I don't want to settle for the first guy that comes along," Rachel whispered.

"I don't want you to settle, Rachel. But, I don't want you to never try because you're afraid. You have to risk getting hurt to find true love."

Rachel spent the rest of the day with her mother. They talked about old times and looked at pictures of her father. For the first time in a long time, they talked like friends. Rachel left for Myerstown with a refreshed spirit and a peace she hadn't known in a long time.

# twenty-one

Randy spent a less-than-restful night. His bedcovers were a mangled mess at the foot of the bed, and his pajamas were beyond wrinkled. He couldn't stop thinking about Rachel and her mother. There was something going on between them that was under the surface, like a volcano waiting to erupt. Rachel's embarrassment had been almost palpable.

Kathryn's unexpected visit hadn't helped his state of mind any, either. There were some complications with the satellite school. Certain officials thought that there were already too many colleges in the state already, especially in this particular area. If the deal fell through, what was he going to do? He couldn't keep working so close to Rachel. Then again, she might be busy at the Center since she would be the director now, but it would be a couple of months before the Center was operational again if Ms. Stanford could pull off the deal. Somehow he knew she would. The woman was like a steamroller. Either one moved out of her way or he or she became a permanent part of the landscape. There was something working below the surface there as well. He could feel it.

Randy stopped for a moment and prayed for Emily Stanford and Rachel, as well as for guidance. He needed all the help he could get these days. With a sigh, he threw back what was left of the covers and headed for the bathroom. Maybe a hot shower would help him think clearer.

❧

The rest of the week went by so fast that Rachel barely remembered it. Her report to Ms. Stanford had put her several days behind on her work at the university, and it took all of Thursday and Friday to finish grading and preparing lessons. She had also neglected her housework, leaving laundry and dishes piled to the ceiling. The nice thing was that she hadn't had time to think about Randy, or Kathryn, or her mother. By the time Sunday afternoon rolled around she was ready for a break. Just as she was dozing off, the telephone rang, causing Rachel to pop straight up on the bed.

"Hello."

"Ms. Grant, this is Ms. Stanford. I need to meet with you this evening to make some final decisions regarding the Center."

"I thought we were meeting tomorrow after my last class."

"Well, there have been some developments that I would like to discuss before tomorrow."

"Are you sure it can't wait?"

"Positive. I'll expect you in half an hour." There was a decisive click on the other end of the phone.

"Nice talking to you, too. Bye," Rachel said into the dead receiver. She hung up the phone with a snap, but it was several moments before she could get the snap back in her body or her brain.

Thirty minutes later she was ringing Ms. Stanford's doorbell. The butler appeared and she followed him into the library where he motioned her to sit in front of the fireplace and then did another of his disappearing acts. As soon as he was gone, she walked around the room, perusing the collection of books. What she wouldn't give for a couple of months in this room. She ran her hands down the piano as she passed. It was a beautiful instrument. Although she didn't play, it had always been a dream of hers to own a grand piano and have a room like this one to put it in. Some pictures in silver frames caught her eye. One was a picture of a young Emily with a handsome young man in uniform. They were staring into each other's eyes.

"That was my Tommy." Rachel whirled around at the sound of Emily Stanford's voice.

"He's very handsome," Rachel replied.

"Was," Emily picked up the picture and ran her hand down the frame.

"The two of you looked very happy."

"We were until the war came." She put the picture down and moved toward the fire. She warmed her hands before the fire.

"What happened?"

"He was killed at Pearl Harbor ten days before our wedding," she replied. Her voice was hard and cold despite the warmth of the fire.

"I'm so sorry. That must have been hard for you."

"The war was hard on everyone," she said, shrugging off Rachel's sympathy. "I made a life for myself, volunteering during the war effort and in charities after the war. I kept myself busy. Now, I have all this." She indicated the room with a sweeping motion. She gave a bitter laugh. "I have all this, but no one to share it with."

"Don't you have friends and family?"

"I'm the last of my family and my so-called friends only want what they can get out of me." The bitterness in her voice gave Rachel a chill. "You'll see someday, my girl. You'll see."

"I thought you wanted to discuss the Center, Ms. Stanford." Rachel changed the subject, unwilling to let this woman's bitterness invade the sense of calm and peace she had recently discovered.

"So I did." She moved to the desk and pulled out a folder. "Here is the deed to the land and the building. The next step is hiring a construction crew to start the renovations. I want them to start tomorrow morning, so I wanted your opinion as to which company gets the job. Here are the bids we received."

Rachel was stunned that the woman had gotten this far in such a short time. Getting the property was one thing, but getting bids from construction companies as well was amazing. Rachel took the folder and opened it. The top sheet was a list of the construction companies and their bids. It was easy to see which was the best offer.

"Well, it's obvious that Wilson Construction should get the deal. They're a well-known firm, and they gave the best bid."

"I agree," Emily said with a nod. "I'll notify Mr. Wilson this evening."

"What else did you need to discuss?"

"That was it."

"You called me over just for that? You could have made that decision without my help, Ms. Stanford."

"This is going to be your show, Ms. Grant. I thought you should have input in all the decisions."

"That's nice of you, but it's not necessary," Rachel replied. "So, I guess you don't need to meet with me tomorrow, then." Rachel turned to go, but Ms. Stanford stopped her.

"On the contrary, we still have things to discuss tomorrow. Be sure to bring your copy of the report with you." She strode across the room in a manner that belied her years. "I'll expect you for lunch." Without another word she swept through the doorway and the butler popped up in her place.

"I'll show you out, Ms. Grant." Knowing that she had been dismissed for the evening, Rachel followed the butler. All the way to the car and on her way home she puzzled over Emily Stanford's behavior. She didn't need Rachel's advice, so why did she insist that Rachel come over tonight and tomorrow? Did she like having someone at her beck and call? She soon dismissed that idea. The woman had plenty of servants and employees to boss. It wasn't until she was going through the mail at home that she came up with another possibility. Emily Stanford was lonely.

The next day went by as usual for a Monday. Her students were late and slow to answer. She wasn't at the top of her game either, for that matter. Everything seemed to move in a slow-motion haze, a reflection of the weather outside. Besides, finals were coming up way too soon. So was the day of Randy's departure. She didn't want to even consider that possibility right now. It might send her over the edge.

As promised, Rachel headed for Ms. Stanford's mansion as soon as classes were over. The butler led her to a smaller dining room where Ms. Stanford was waiting, a maid hovering in the background.

"There you are. I was beginning to think you weren't coming." Rachel detected a note of displeasure in her voice.

"I got here as soon as I could, Ms. Stanford."

"Well, never mind. Sit down and Mary will serve lunch."

Rachel obeyed. Looking at the place setting, she noticed there were more pieces of cutlery than she was used to. She wasn't even sure what some of them were. The maid served lunch one course at a time, coming in at intervals to take away their dirty dishes. Their lunch was eaten with only the sound of the fork and knife hitting the china. Emily Stanford was queen of this castle to be sure. Rachel was relieved when they left the table and returned to the library. At least there she had some notion as to how to behave.

Ms. Stanford seemed reluctant to start their discussion. She insisted that they have coffee before they started, and took tiny sips from her cup. Finally, an hour into their visit, she mentioned the Center.

"Would you mind bringing me the folder from the desk? It has the designs Mr. Wilson brought me this morning."

Rachel did as requested, taking a quick peek at the designs before handing the folder to Ms. Stanford. She motioned for Rachel to take the seat next to her on the couch.

"This is a picture of the building in 1950." It was as Rachel had always imagined it. The weathered bricks were set off by freshly painted shutters in white.

"That's exactly how I thought it would look," Rachel exclaimed.

"I had hoped you would feel this way. I told Mr. Wilson that I wanted it restored to its original beauty. They just don't make buildings like this anymore." She sighed and replaced the picture. In that moment Rachel caught a glimpse of the young girl from the picture on the piano.

"I really love old buildings. When I go on vacation, I always take more pictures of buildings than I do of people." Rachel smiled and received a small smile in return. She could see a chink in Ms. Stanford's armor, her Achilles' heel.

"I used to draw when I was a girl, and my mother was always scolding me for drawing buildings instead of landscapes or portraits." Rachel waited for her to continue. "I always wanted to design houses and buildings, but girls didn't do that sort of thing when I was growing up."

Rachel could see some of the bitterness bubbling to the surface once again. There had been a lot of disappointment in Emily's life. But there was still time for change.

"May I call you Emily?" Rachel asked, and the woman seemed taken aback by the request.

"I don't see why not," she finally said, after a long pause. "Then, I'll call you Rachel."

"Great. Now what else is there to discuss?" Rachel asked.

"That was it. I just wanted to make sure you approved." Emily picked an invisible piece of lint from her spotless suit.

"Well, in that case, I'd better be going. I have to get ready for finals." Rachel stood. "I'll see you next Monday, same time."

"Yes, of course. Next Monday." Emily nodded her approval.

This time the butler didn't see her out. She found the door with no problem and headed home with a smile. So it was Rachel and Emily now. She smiled even brighter at the thought. She had just made a new friend.

# twenty-two

Randy looked at the completed master bedroom. He should have felt a sense of satisfaction, but he felt oddly disappointed. It wouldn't be complete until it had furniture, but that would be for the new owners to decide. A real estate agent was coming by in an hour. He had spent the weekend putting the finishing touches on the house. It was finished, but empty. Even if he didn't change jobs, he couldn't stay in this house alone. It was meant for a family and kids, not a lonely bachelor.

The doorbell rang, a welcome interruption to his reverie. That had to be the realtor. He walked downstairs, anxious for this to be over with and yet hesitant. He'd hate to see this house go. Opening the door, he found a pouty Kathryn fidgeting on his steps. She pushed past him into the house.

"So this is where you've been spending all your time."

He ignored her opening line. "What are you doing here, Kathryn?"

"Can't a girl come and visit her brother?" Kathryn gave him that innocent look that so often got her her own way.

"Considering I've lived here for over a year and you've never been to my house, no." He crossed his arms over his chest and waited.

"There's no sense dancing around it. I got the news this morning. The satellite project has been cancelled permanently."

"Why?" Randy asked, though he already knew the answer.

"The university decided there weren't enough possible students to warrant the expense of renting the buildings and hiring more teachers." She kicked at the floor with the toe of her four-inch heels. "I was so looking forward to having you closer to home."

"I am home, Kathryn. This is my home."

"Not for long, I understand," she said, eyeing him suspiciously.

"What do you mean?" Randy asked. She was up to something. He could tell by the look in her eyes.

"I heard that you're putting the house up for sale. What's up with that, big brother?" She crossed her arms and tapped one shoe.

"I only bought this house as an investment. I finished the remodeling and now I'm going to sell it for a profit. Any other questions?"

"Why don't I believe you?" Kathryn asked.

"I don't know. I'm not a mind reader."

"Neither am I, big brother, but I do know you, and this isn't like you. You were so excited when you bought this house, talking about a wife and kids and a dog in the backyard. Now, here you are bailing out when it's just finished. It doesn't add up." She looked up at him, a smug expression on her face. "What gives?"

"I don't know what you're talking about."

"Come on. I know there's something wrong." She paused for a moment and then asked, "What's her name?"

He jumped at her question, and he could tell by the look on her face that he'd been caught. He decided to play dumb.

"I don't know what you're talking about."

"That's the third time you've said that."

"Well, you ask a silly question, and you get a silly answer, no matter how many times you ask it." She crossed the room and put a hand on his arm.

"I know there's something bothering you, Randy. Please tell me. I can't help you if you don't tell me what the problem is." His shoulders slumped at the worried look in her eyes.

"You couldn't help anyway, sis, but thanks for the offer."

"So, it is a woman. What's her name?"

"Rachel."

"That's a pretty name. Who is she?" Kathryn asked.

"She's a teacher at the university. She used to be one of my students." Once he started talking, it was like a flood was released. He told Kathryn all about her, and her jerk of a boyfriend. They settled at the kitchen table and she listened until he had finished.

"Did you pray about it?" Kathryn was always one to get to the point.

"Yes."

"And. . ." She waited for him to finish.

"And He said wait."

"Then why are you jumping off the deep end and selling this house?"

"What do you mean?" Randy asked, his brow wrinkling in confusion.

"I mean, He told you to wait, not to give up. Maybe she just needs a little time to realize what a jerk her boyfriend is and what a great guy you are."

"But they're engaged," Randy replied. "They must be in love."

"Don't be so naïve, Randy. Remember Danny." Danny had been one of Kathryn's first boyfriends. "He asked me to marry him and I said yes, but it didn't take me long to figure out that it wouldn't work. I only said yes because he was the first guy to ask me."

"So, you think she might be having second thoughts."

"If the guy is as big a jerk as you say, and she's as smart as you say, then I'm sure she has. You'd be doing her a favor by getting her away from this guy before it's too late. Besides, you said that she said something about not wanting you to move. . .seems like a pretty big hint to me."

"She has seemed kind of upset lately. Maybe she is having second thoughts about this guy." He felt his spirits lift at the thought. "What should I do, Kathryn? I can't just go up and ask her. I have to find out how she feels about the jerk without making a fool of myself."

"If you love her enough, isn't it worth making a fool

out of yourself?" Kathryn asked.

Randy thought about it for a moment. If it meant winning Rachel, he didn't care what kind of a fool he looked like, but if it meant ruining their friendship forever, then Kathryn could just forget it. She gave a sigh.

"Okay. Why don't you ask her friends about their relationship?"

"I don't know any of her friends."

"Well I suggest that you find out or ask her point-blank."

"You always were tough as nails, sis." He smiled at her and tugged a golden curl.

"I have another suggestion," Kathryn said. Randy eyed her carefully.

"What's that?"

"Tell the realtor to take a hike." Randy smiled.

After Kathryn left, the realtor arrived. Randy chose a more polite way to tell the realtor that he had changed his mind. He closed the door and leaned on it. For some reason the house didn't seem quite so empty. He could almost hear little feet on the stairs.

The sound of the wind whipping through the trees reminded him of the tornado and the Center. What was Rachel's friend's name from the Center? Sherry. No. Sarah. No. Susan. That was it! Susan. He hit the banister in triumph. Tomorrow he would talk to Susan.

# twenty-three

Rachel watched as the work crew threw the damaged shingles onto the growing heap. Just a couple of weeks ago a wrecking ball was stationed right at this spot. Now, a group of men were struggling to repair the damage done by the tornado and by time. It was like watching a resurrection take place, something new out of the old. She was standing on the threshold of a new era in her life. What was she going to do? She released a deep sigh. Maybe she was meant to work in full-time service instead of getting married. In the Bible, Paul said that single people could devote more of their time to the Lord.

Walking back to her car, Rachel pondered the thought. With a hesitant heart, she looked up beyond the fluffy clouds and made a decision.

"Lord, I want to do your will, and if that means not getting married, then that's what I want," she whispered sincerely.

She felt the wind against her face, and it was almost as if a hand brushed the fear away. She could feel God's presence in this place. She belonged here, not at the university. Here she could make a difference in someone's life. At the university, she was just another teacher, and not a very good one, at that. She hated grading papers and making tests. What she loved was working with these women and children and giving them not just the skills they needed, but the encouragement as well. This was home. Here she would never really be alone.

She got into her car and headed for her apartment, but something drew her to Emily's house. "What, Lord? What do you want me to do?" she prayed.

*"Just go."*

"I don't know what to say."

*"I'll give you the words."*

"I'm afraid."

*"I'll give you strength."*

"I'll try, Father."

*"That's all I ask."*

She pulled into the Stanford driveway and parked in what was becoming her usual space. This time when the butler answered, he just motioned toward the library and disappeared. Rachel waited with her hand on the doorknob and took a deep breath. She rapped lightly on the paneled door and heard a quiet, "Come in." Emily was sitting on the couch holding the picture of Tommy in his uniform.

"I hope I'm not intruding," Rachel began.

"No, not at all," Emily said, trying to regain her composure. The red, puffy eyes told that she had been crying, though her ramrod-straight back dared anyone to argue with her. "What can I do for you?"

"Actually, I came to ask what I could do for you, Emily."

She looked startled. "What do you mean?"

"I just had a feeling that I should come to see you today, that you needed to talk to someone."

"I can't imagine why you would think that." She pulled the picture closer to her chest.

"To tell the truth, Emily, God told me to come here today."

"God." Rachel heard the sarcasm in her voice. "What does God care about me?"

"He cares very much for you, Emily. He always has." Rachel saw the bitterness finally boiling toward the surface—it was making Emily's life miserable. Rachel prayed for the right words to help.

"He has a funny way of showing it." She stood abruptly and faced the fireplace. The grate was empty because of the warm weather, but ashes remained from something recently burned. "As a child, I was faithful to church and Sunday school. I did what was right according to the Bible, even when it wasn't popular. I prayed and read my Bible every day. What did I get for my trouble? This!"

Rachel could see it was a faded telegram. Though Rachel couldn't read it, she knew it must be the notice of Tommy's death. Emily clutched the telegram tightly in her hand and shook it up into the air.

"This is what I got in return. If God loved me so much, why did he let my Tommy die? I prayed every night that he would come home safe to me. He wasn't even in the front lines. Why did this have to happen? Why?"

"I don't know why, Emily. Bad things happen every day, but it's not God's choice. People make choices that affect other people."

"He could have stopped it."

"Yes, He has the power to stop it, but in His love for us, He gave us free will." Rachel crossed the room and laid a hand on Emily's arm. "I don't know why Tommy died, but I do know that He let you live. There's a reason for that, Emily."

"Why?" Emily asked. The tears began to stream down her cheeks, and a sob rose from somewhere deep within. "Why? Why am I still alive? What purpose is there for an old spinster like me?"

Rachel could see the pain and loneliness in her eyes. She put an arm around her shoulders and pulled her close. "That's between you and God, Emily. But, I know if we pray about it, God will answer."

"How can you be sure?" Emily asked hesitantly.

"Because He is faithful, Emily, even when we aren't. Whenever I ask, He always answers. Not always in the way that I want Him to, but He always answers." Rachel took Emily's hands in hers. "Let's pray. You tell God all your pain and fears, and ask Him for His help."

Emily nodded her head, too broken to answer. They bowed their heads and prayed. A little while later, Rachel left a more peaceful Emily alone with her God.

Rachel's step was lighter than it had been in months. She skipped her way up the sidewalk and into the apartment. Finals started tomorrow and then school would be out for the summer, but she would be out for good. Somewhere between the Center and Emily's, Rachel had decided to quit her job at the university. The time she had spent with Emily just confirmed her suspicions that she was meant to work at the Center full time. She wasn't sure what that would mean financially, but God would take care of the details. This was His plan, not hers.

❧

Randy found Susan totally by accident. He walked into The Magnolia so lost in thought that he almost ran over her.

"Excuse me," he muttered, moving past her toward his table.

"Hey, aren't you Randy Harris? From the English department?"

"Yes. Do I know you?" Randy asked.

"Not exactly. My name's Susan Peterson. I'm a friend of Rachel Grant's. Do you happen to know where I can find Rachel?" Susan asked.

"I know she's already left for the day. Is there a problem?"

"No. I just thought she might like to have a cup of tea with me." She looked disappointed, even concerned.

"I was just about to have a cup myself. Would you like to join me?" Randy offered her his arm. She took it as they walked to his favorite spot. The spot he'd first sat at with Rachel. He took a deep breath and then plunged in.

"I'm afraid I've asked you to tea with a hidden agenda. I need to ask you something which you may tell me is none of my business." Randy stopped to clear his throat. He was starting to ramble. He could tell by her bemused expression. "I mean, that is to say. . ."

"Spit it out, Dr. Harris."

"Is Rachel really in love with Kyle?" he blurted out. Susan's mouth dropped open. "Never mind. It's really none of my business." He started to stand up and make a hasty exit, but she grabbed him by the arm and pulled him back into his chair with a thud.

"Are you in love with Rachel?" When he refused to answer, he could tell she knew the truth. "You are. This is great!" She clapped her hands in delight.

"What do you mean great? It's a mess." She looked puzzled.

"What are you talking about? It's perfect."

"How can it be perfect when she's engaged to Kyle?" he asked.

"Engaged to Kyle? Where did you hear that?" Susan looked stunned.

"From Kyle."

"When did he tell you that?" Susan asked.

"The week after the tornado. He came by looking for her and said they were engaged."

"They were never engaged. She dumped him like a hot potato weeks ago," Susan cried. "The jerk. I can't believe he said that."

Randy stared at her for several moments. "You mean

they only dated a few times?"

"Yes. She found out what a real jerk he was and told him off." Susan sat up straight in her chair. "Is that why you suddenly decided to move south?" Randy nodded.

"I'm not going anymore, though. The project was cancelled. I got the news yesterday."

"That's great." Susan grasped his arm. "Not because you didn't get the promotion, but great that you're staying."

"I understand, but now what do I do?" Randy patted her arm.

"You go talk to her."

"Easier said than done." They finished their tea, punctuated by playful slaps from Susan. She was chattering happily about the good news, but he wasn't listening too closely.

He left Susan at the door of The Magnolia and headed for home. He needed time to think this through. He didn't want to make any more stupid mistakes. Once inside the house, he went to his special place, a window seat that overlooked the backyard. He bowed his head and quieted his heart.

*Lord, what should I do?*

*"Go to her."*

*What do I say?*

*"Tell her the truth."*

*What if she doesn't want me?*

He prayed for a few more moments, but he knew what he had to do. He had to find out for himself. He had to be willing to take the risk of rejection. Randy prayed for guidance, for the right words, as he never had before. At last a gentle peace flooded his soul. He looked out the window. The sun was beginning to set, and tomorrow was a new day.

# twenty-four

The rest of the week went by in a blur of finals and grading, but on Friday morning Rachel turned in her grades and her resignation. She was in her classroom, sorting through what belonged to the university and what belonged to her when Randy stopped by.

"What's going on? Spring cleaning?" Randy asked, eyebrows raised. She was going to miss that expression. She swallowed the lump in her throat.

"More like cleaning out. I just turned in my resignation." Rachel could see the shock in his eyes.

"Why?" He looked puzzled, even hurt. She couldn't imagine why. He would be leaving soon as well.

"I'm the new director of the community center, remember? It's going to be a full-time job. Emily and I have a lot of plans for the place."

"Emily? You mean Ms. Stanford?" He really looked confused now.

"Yes. We've become good friends over the last week or so. Sort of kindred spirits. Besides, I really prefer the work at the Center to teaching at the university. There's a lot more freedom there."

"Oh." He seemed to be struggling to say something.

"Was there something you wanted?" Rachel questioned.

"Yes. Oh yeah." Randy stuttered. "I wanted you to come to my house for dinner tonight. I finally finished remodeling the house and I wanted you to see it."

"Oh, I'd love to see it." Rachel tried to control her enthusiasm. He probably just wanted to show the house to someone. That's all. "What time?"

"About six o'clock?"

"Sounds fine to me. I'll see you then."

Randy nodded and gave a little wave as he rounded the corner. She took a deep breath to steady her nerves. Steady, girl. He has a job down south, and you have a job at the Center. It could never work out. Just calm down. With a sigh, she threw herself into cleaning.

By five-thirty she had convinced herself not to expect anything special tonight. But she couldn't help trying to look her best. Her room looked like the day after a tornado. She had been through every outfit she owned, twice. She settled on a navy pantsuit, not too dressy, but not too casual either. People said the color set off her eyes and hair. With one last look in the mirror, she tucked a stray hair into the French twist and grabbed her car keys. She arrived at Randy's house at a quarter to six. Better early than late. She rang the doorbell and heard a clatter in the background. It was several minutes before Randy appeared. His hair was still damp from the shower.

"You're early," he gasped.

"Are you all right?"

"Fine, fine." He had a distracted air about him.

"Aren't you going to invite me in?"

"Hmm. No. I can't."

"What?" Rachel asked. What was going on here?

"You can't come in until six o'clock." Randy's tall frame filled the doorway so that she couldn't see around him. He was not going to budge.

"Then what do you expect me to do?" Rachel asked, hands on hips. "Sit on the porch?"

"Yes. That's a wonderful idea." He smiled and shut the door. She heard the deadbolt click into place. She stared at the door for several minutes, but he didn't return to let her in. She looked around and spied a swing at the corner of the porch. It hadn't been there the last time she was here. She tested it before she sat down. The faint squeaking soothed her ragged nerves until she relaxed against the swing, reveling in the gentle breeze. At six o'clock on the dot, Randy reappeared at the door.

"Hi, Rachel, glad you could come. Why don't you come in and sit down?" He was pretending as though nothing had happened before. She didn't know what he was up to, but two could play this game.

"I'd love to. Thanks for inviting me."

She followed him into the parlor, but couldn't get past the threshold. Not only had he finished the wallpapering, he had also decorated the room in a rich wine. Beautiful drapes with real lace sheers graced the double window. The Queen Anne couches were covered in the same material with matching wing chairs scattered in clusters around the room.

"Would you care to sit down?" he asked.

She took a seat at the couch, bewildered by his sudden formality. Something was definitely up. He joined her on the couch and motioned toward a tray of spinach dip and vegetables. She took a bite.

"This is my favorite dip," she exclaimed. "How did you know?"

"I didn't know it was your favorite. Small world." He smiled a little too brightly. She noticed his hair was dry and lying in waves over his head. She buried the urge to run her fingers through it and took another bite to cover her nervousness.

"I thought you promised me a tour of the house."

"After dinner. I don't want the food to get cold. Let's go to the dining room." He motioned for her to go first. When she headed for the kitchen, he led her gently in the other direction. "I thought we would eat in the dining room for a change."

"I didn't think you had a table."

"I do now." That was an understatement. A beautiful rosewood table was surrounded by matching chairs covered in a cream brocade. The hardwood floor was covered with a beautiful area rug. The set was completed by a matching buffet and hutch.

"It's beautiful," Rachel gasped.

"I'm glad you like it." He seemed very pleased by her compliment.

"The table setting is beautiful too."

The table was set with matching cream linens and the

centerpiece was a vase of cream-colored roses mixed with deeper wine roses. There were lit candles on both ends of the table, but the places were set at the head of the table. Randy held one of the chairs for her.

"I'll be right back." He went into the kitchen, making sure he closed the swinging door behind him. A few moments later he returned with the salad.

"Let's pray." He blessed the food and they made it through the first course and the main course without a hitch. Randy kept up the small talk about finals and his renovations, but Rachel could tell that there was something he wasn't saying.

"I'll get dessert." He stood and placed the folded napkin next to his plate.

"Let me help you." Rachel pushed her chair back to stand up.

"No!" he shouted. Then he lowered his voice. "I mean, I can take care of it. You're my guest." He gave a little bow and a sheepish smile and backed into the kitchen. A loud crash and the sound of breaking glass sent Rachel scurrying into the kitchen.

"Are you all right?" She pushed open the door to find Randy surrounded by take-out boxes from their favorite Italian restaurant and a tempting chocolate mousse lying at his feet.

"I'm fine, just a case of butterfingers. Just go back and sit down and I'll take care of everything." He waved her toward the dining room, but she ignored him.

"I will not. You stay right where you are. You'll only

make it worse. Where are your cleaning supplies?"

"In the closet under the stairs." He looked like a little boy caught with his hand in the cookie jar. She tried to hide the smile that jerked at the corners of her mouth.

"I'll be right back. Don't move," she warned, pointing her finger at him until he nodded in agreement. She found everything she needed and entered the kitchen from the hall.

"Here, let me." He held out his hand for the dustpan and broom, but she moved them out of his reach.

"No. I've got to get the mousse up before it starts to melt." With a practiced twist she used what was left of the platter to scoop the soggy mess into the trash can. Then she carefully brushed the glass from his shoes and wiped up the remains of the mousse before trying to sweep up the broken shards.

"I can take it from here. Thanks." She handed him the broom, but kept the dustpan.

"I'll hold while you sweep." She looked up at him with a smile. His face was flushed and he merely nodded. She emptied the rest of the glass into the trash can and stood up. "You'll probably need to sweep again very carefully and then mop so that the mousse doesn't make the floor sticky."

"I'll take care of that later. Why don't you go sit in the parlor and I'll bring the coffee."

"Why don't I help you clean the table and the kitchen?" Rachel offered.

"No. I'll take care of it later."

"It won't take long." She walked into the dining room as she talked. "I can clear the table and you can start in the kitchen."

He grabbed her arm. "No. I don't want you to help clean. You're a guest. Please have a seat in the parlor and I'll bring the coffee." His face was still flushed, but she could tell he was getting agitated.

"Okay." She shook her head. "I'll meet you in the parlor."

He watched her walk out of the room, making sure she was really gone. As she took her place on the sofa, she wondered what was wrong with him tonight. Maybe he had decided that he needed to explain about the kiss, let her know he had a girlfriend. Her face warmed at the very thought. The last thing she needed was a "talk," the old "let's just be friends" routine. She thought about leaving right now while he was still in the kitchen, but she knew that would be rude.

Randy returned with the silver service a few moments later and set it up on the coffee table. "Cream or sugar?"

"Both. I like a little coffee with my cream and sugar," she quipped. He smiled and seemed to relax. "You know, this is the first time I've ever seen anyone use a coffee table for serving coffee." He laughed.

"Me too, come to think about it." He handed her a dainty cup and saucer. When he picked up his own, she was surprised at how easily he held the cup in his hands and yet he still looked so masculine. His large hands were well-worn from work, but they were gentle with the fragile china. She wondered what it would feel like in his arms, to have those hands holding hers. She shook the image away.

"Are you cold?" he asked, immediately concerned. "I can turn up the heat."

"No. No, I'm fine. Just a shiver."

"Are you sure?"

"I'm positive," she assured him. The last thing she needed was more heat right now. She could feel her face beginning to burn. She sipped her coffee, unsure what to say. He did the same. When she had finally swallowed the last drop, she put the cup down on the table.

"Would you like another cup?" he offered, reaching for the coffee.

"No. One cup is all I need this late."

"Oh, of course. I should have made decaf." He looked disappointed.

"I believe you were going to give me a tour of the rest of the house," she said, relieved to have something to do besides sit and stare at her coffee cup. This was so unlike Randy.

"Yes, I was. Let me show you the rest of the downstairs." He gave her a guided tour of the other rooms, noting what he had done. They were all as beautiful as the parlor. The den was void of furniture except a television and a recliner.

"What are you going to do in here?" Rachel asked.

"I'm going to buy some lived-in furniture for this room. I consider this to be the place where the real living is done. A place for a family to gather and watch television or play games or just talk. What do you think?" He looked at her as though he were judging her answers very carefully.

"I think that's a great idea. You wouldn't want children climbing on those antiques in the parlor."

"Exactly. This is a room for kids to play in or adults to put their feet up on." He smiled in a way that made him seem very satisfied. She passed the test whatever it was. She tried not to imagine Kathryn and Randy curled up on a sofa in front of the couch. "Now, let me show you upstairs."

He took her through all the rooms, most of them still devoid of furniture, except the one where he slept. It only had a bed frame and a dresser. He stopped in front of the master bedroom for a moment and then turned around.

"I saved this room for last because I took your advice about the colors and I wanted your opinion on the finished project."

He opened the door and she gasped in surprise. The room was exactly as she had described it. He had even put up the window treatments she had suggested and a new comforter and sheet set were sitting on the ladder-back chair. The chair was the only piece of furniture in the room.

"Where's the bed?" she asked.

"Well, I think a bedroom suite is something a man and wife should pick out together. Don't you?" She could feel his eyes on her back, waiting for a reaction.

"Of course." She swallowed the lump in her throat. He was asking for more advice. He probably still felt insecure in his relationship with Kathryn. "I'm sure Kathryn will love shopping for this room."

"Why would I want Kathryn to pick out the furniture?" he asked. She turned around to look at Randy. He looked truly puzzled.

"When you get married, of course. She'll want to pick out the furniture."

"My wife would pick out the furniture, not Kathryn." Randy ran a hand through his hair, obviously frustrated. Then he looked up at her, and he snapped his fingers. "You think I'm marrying Kathryn." It was a statement, not a question.

"Well, aren't you?" Rachel asked.

"No. Kathryn's my sister." Randy's smile went from ear to ear.

"Then, if you aren't marrying Kathryn, who's picking out the furniture?"

"You are, you silly woman," Randy said, the grin getting wider by the minute. "Why do you think I brought you over here tonight? Why do you think I had this room decorated to your exact description?"

"I don't know," Rachel said, dizzied by what he was saying.

"I did it because I love you, Rachel Grant, and I want you to help me fill this house with love, and furniture, and children." He crossed the room and grasped her shoulders firmly in both hands. "Will you marry me?"

Rachel stared into his eyes and began to shake. He pulled her closer into his arms to hold her steady.

"Rachel?" he questioned. She stared at him in shock until he shook her firmly. "Rachel, are you all right? Speak to me." She took a deep shaky breath.

"Yes."

"Yes, you're all right, or yes, you'll marry me?"

"Yes to both questions." He hesitated about a second before he took her in his arms and kissed her. It felt like home.

# A Letter To Our Readers

Dear Reader:

In order that we might better contribute to your reading enjoyment, we would appreciate your taking a few minutes to respond to the following questions. We welcome your comments and read each form and letter we receive. When completed, please return to the following:

Rebecca Germany, Fiction Editor
Heartsong Presents
PO Box 719
Uhrichsville, Ohio 44683

1. Did you enjoy reading *The Plan?*
   ❑ Very much. I would like to see more books by this author!
   ❑ Moderately
   I would have enjoyed it more if ________________

   ________________________________

   ________________________________

2. Are you a member of **Heartsong Presents**? Yes ❑ No ❑
   If no, where did you purchase this book?______________

   ________________________________

3. How would you rate, on a scale from 1 (poor) to 5 (superior), the cover design?______________________

4. On a scale from 1 (poor) to 10 (superior), please rate the following elements.

   _____ Heroine　　_____ Plot

   _____ Hero　　_____ Inspirational theme

   _____ Setting　　_____ Secondary characters

5. These characters were special because________________

________________________________________

________________________________________

6. How has this book inspired your life?________________

________________________________________

________________________________________

7. What settings would you like to see covered in future **Heartsong Presents** books?________________

________________________________________

________________________________________

8. What are some inspirational themes you would like to see treated in future books?________________

________________________________________

________________________________________

9. Would you be interested in reading other **Heartsong Presents** titles? Yes ❑ No ❑

10. Please check your age range:

❑ Under 18 ❑ 18-24 ❑ 25-34
❑ 35-45 ❑ 46-55 ❑ Over 55

11. How many hours per week do you read?________________

Name ____________________________________

Occupation ________________________________

Address __________________________________

City ____________ State ________ Zip ________

# *Women in touch with God!*

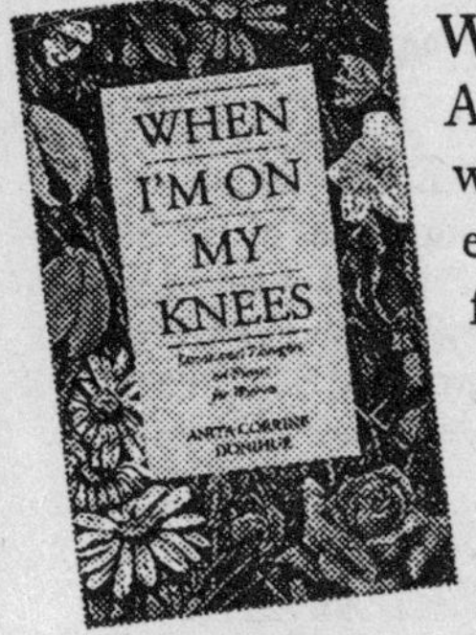


## When I'm On My Knees

A compilation of prayers from a woman's point of view, prayers that emanate from the heart, prayers about friendship, family, and peace. 224 pages, Printed Leatherette, 4 3/16" x 6 3/4"

## When I'm Praising God

This follow-up to the highly-popular book, *When I'm On My Knees*, will encourage women to praise God in any and every situation. A heart-felt collection of prayers, devotional thoughts, poems, and Scripture, *When I'm Praising God* can help readers turn even the trials of life into victories. 224 pages, Printed Leatherette, 4 3/16" x 6 3/4"

Please send me ____ copies of *When I'm On My Knees, and* ____ copies of *When I'm Praising God*. I am enclosing $4.97 each. (Please add $1.00 to cover postage and handling per order. OH add 6% tax.)

Send check or money order, no cash or C.O.D.s please.

Name________________________________________

Address______________________________________

City, State, Zip _______________________________

**To place a credit card order, call 1-800-847-8270.**

**Send to:** Heartsong Presents Reader Service, PO Box 719, Uhrichsville, OH 44683

# Presents

_HP269 WALKING THE DOG, *Gail Sattler*
_HP270 PROMISE ME FOREVER, *Andrea Boeshaar*
_HP273 SUMMER PLACE, *Peggy Darty*
_HP274 THE HEALING PROMISE, *Hannah Alexander*
_HP277 ONCE MORE WITH FEELING, *Brenda Bancroft*
_HP278 ELIZABETH'S CHOICE, *Linda Lyle*
_HP281 WILD IRISH ROSES, *Una McManus*
_HP282 THE WEDDING WISH, *Loree Lough*
_HP289 THE PERFECT WIFE, *Gina Fields*
_HP290 AFTER THE STORM, *Yvonne Lehman*
_HP293 A SENSE OF PLACE, *Veda Boyd Jones*
_HP294 TO TRULY SEE, *Kristin Billerbeck*
_HP297 A THOUSAND HILLS, *Ranee McCollum*
_HP298 A SENSE OF BELONGING, *Terry Fowler*
_HP301 SECOND TIME AROUND, *Andrea Boeshaar*
_HP302 SEASONS, *Gail Gaymer Martin*
_HP305 CALL OF THE MOUNTAIN, *Yvonne Lehman*
_HP306 PIANO LESSONS, *Gail Sattler*
_HP309 PRIZE PACKAGE, *Catherine Runyon*
_HP310 THE RELUCTANT BRIDE, *Helen Spears*
_HP313 SEALED WITH A KISS, *Loree Lough*
_HP314 SEA ESCAPE, *Lynn A. Coleman*
_HP317 LOVE REMEMBERED, *Ann Bell*
_HP318 BORN FOR THIS LOVE, *Brenda Bancroft*
_HP321 FORTRESS OF LOVE, *Melanie Panagiotopoulos*
_HP322 COUNTRY CHARM, *DiAnn Mills*
_HP325 GONE CAMPING, *Gail Sattler*
_HP326 A TENDER MELODY, *Birdie L. Etchison*
_HP329 MEET MY SISTER, TESS, *Kristin Billerbeck*
_HP330 DREAMING OF CASTLES, *Gail Gaymer Martin*
_HP333 BEHIND THE MASK, *Lauralee Bliss*
_HP334 ESCAPE, *Kathleen Paul*
_HP337 OZARK SUNRISE, *Hannah Alexander*
_HP338 SOMEWHERE A RAINBOW, *Yvonne Lehman*
_HP341 IT ONLY TAKES A SPARK, *Pamela Kaye Tracy*
_HP342 THE HAVEN OF REST, *Andrea Boeshaar*
_HP345 THE PLAN, *Linda Lyle*
_HP346 DOUBLE TAKE, *Terry Fowler*

## Great Inspirational Romance at a Great Price!

**Heartsong Presents** books are inspirational romances in contemporary and historical settings, designed to give you an enjoyable, spirit-lifting reading experience. You can choose wonderfully written titles from some of today's best authors like Veda Boyd Jones, Yvonne Lehman, Tracie Peterson, Debra White Smith, and many others.

***When ordering quantities less than twelve, above titles are $2.95 each.***
***Not all titles may be available at time of order.***

SEND TO: **Heartsong Presents** Reader's Service
P.O. Box 719, Uhrichsville, Ohio 44683

Please send me the items checked above. I am enclosing $________
(please add $1.00 to cover postage per order. OH add 6.25% tax. NJ add 6%.). Send check or money order, no cash or C.O.D.s, please.
**To place a credit card order, call 1-800-847-8270.**

**NAME** ______________________________

**ADDRESS** ______________________________

**CITY/STATE** ______________________ **ZIP** ________

HPS 10-99